9/10/21 $ 3.75

RIDING THE HEAVENS

STORIES AND ADVENTURES
TO INSPIRE YOUR FAITH

RIDING THE HEAVENS

STORIES AND ADVENTURES
TO INSPIRE YOUR FAITH

MAX MEYERS

ZondervanPublishingHouse
Grand Rapids, Michigan 49530
http://www.zondervan.com

Riding the Heavens
Copyright © 2000 by Max Meyers

Requests for information should be addressed to:

 ZondervanPublishingHouse
Grand Rapids, Michigan 49530

Library of Congress Cataloging-in-Publication Data

Meyers, Max, 1955-
    Riding the heavens : stories and adventures to inspire your faith / Max Meyers.
      p. cm.
    Includes bibliographical references.
    ISBN 0-310-23333-X (hardcover : alk. paper)
    1. Meyers, Max, 1955- 2. Mission Aviation Fellowship–Biography. 3. Aeronautics in missionary work I. Title.
    BV2082.A9 2000
    266'.0092—dc21   99-059300
    [B]   CIP

This edition printed on acid-free paper.

Published in association with the literary agency of Alive Communications, Inc., 1465 Kelly Johnson Blvd. #320, Colorado Springs, CO 80920

Interior design by Amy E. Langeler

Printed in the United States of America

---

00 01 02 03 04 05 /❖ DC/ 10 9 8 7 6 5 4 3 2 1

···Contents···

Part One

1. A Higher Plane   11
2. Doubts   17
3. Two Small Sticks   27
4. Why?   31

Part Two

5. Hope on a River's Edge   37
6. Triumph and Tragedy at Tifalmin   45
7. The Compassionate Cannibal   55
8. No-Nonsense Faithfulness   61
9. Skin-Deep Fear   69
10. Of Cows, Cans, and Communion Wine   73

Part Three

11. War   87
12. Light Over Darkness   93
13. Timbuktu   99
14. An Albanian Named Jimmy   107

Part Four

15. Boyhood   117
16. The Lostness of the Lost   123
17. The Invisible Communion   131
18. I Will Take Him from Here   141

A Note from the Author   147

There is no one like the God of Jeshurun,
who rides on the heavens to help you
and on the clouds in his majesty.
The eternal God is your refuge,
and underneath are the everlasting arms.

DEUTERONOMY 33: 26–27

PART ONE

Chapter One

···A Higher Plane···

When I consider your heavens,
the work of your fingers,
the moon and the stars,
which you have set in place,
what is man that you are
mindful of him,
the son of man that
you care for him.

PSALM 8:3–4

The sky was to be mine alone that night.

Tanks brimming with fuel, my Gloucester Meteor Mk VIII jet fighter sat low and heavy, its military-gray coat a perfect camouflage against the winter's night. I fumbled with my flashlight. The rain and wind made preflight inspection difficult and uncomfortable.

Releasing the bubble canopy, I climbed into the airplane and settled into my seat.

After the customary check around the cockpit and a "thumbs-up" to the waiting crew chief, I flipped the starter switch for the left-hand engine and listened for the reassuring whine of the compressor. The instruments flickered into life—RPM, oil pressure, jet-pipe temperature, fuel flow. Anticipating the unmistakable deep-throated rumble of ignition, I repeated the procedure on the right engine. With the wheel chocks removed, all was ready.

I could not have known that this rather routine flight would give rise to a most memorable experience.

The penetrating beam of the nose light pierced the darkness and illuminated the driving rain. I followed the diffused lights of the taxiway into the night. Completing the final memorized checklist "on the run" and positioning the aircraft on the runway centerline, I held it stationary with the brakes.

I opened the throttles with my left hand and gripped the brake lever with my right. The two jet engines responded with a familiar, throaty roar as the power increased. The airplane strained, eager to fly. Exhilaration. Energy brought to life with the left hand, held captive with the right.

Taking a breath, I released the brakes, and like a sprinter from the blocks, the airplane leaped forward, pressing me back: 75 knots . . . 90 knots . . . ease back on the column . . . nose wheel off . . . 120 knots . . . airborne . . . undercarriage retracted . . . climbing speed.

I began scanning the instruments and in a matter of seconds was enveloped by heavy clouds, immediately encountering the violent buffeting and turbulence that gives thunderstorms their notoriety amongst aviators. The ferocity of the storm surprised me. My three-ton aircraft was being tossed and thrown about. I marveled at the energy and power of just one winter storm. Not a good night to fly!

Suddenly, at thirty-five thousand feet I burst into the blackness above the clouds.

The night sky was brilliantly clear. The stars were clusters of bright light. It seemed I could reach out and clutch them, one by one. Below, the earth was totally obscured by a soft pewter-gray blanket of cloud. With the stars as my close and sole companions, I turned onto heading, my frustrations with the weather gone, my regrets forgotten.

Soon I was hard at work, leaving the stars to their own beauty. I concentrated on the task of successfully completing what was a navigational exercise.

Fifty minutes later, high over the western reaches of Australia's New South Wales, the exercise was finished. I had reached the third and final checkpoint on time and with reasonable accuracy. It was now simply a matter of flying home. The pressure was off. It was time to relax!

Heading east, I looked up through the clear canopy to survey again the beauty of the night sky. Tuning the radio from the repetitive "dots and dashes" of the navigational beacons I had been using, I found a pleasant, all-night classical music station. With the roar of the engines left far behind, the soft and lovely strains of a string quartet somehow matched the night!

But my memory of that night was to change forever. It was barely discernible at first. Far ahead, increasing in intensity as the minutes ticked by, a blood-red horizontal line appeared against the blackness of the sky.

Away to the south I noticed another line, that same brilliant red, not straight like the first but curled and irregular, arching high into the atmosphere.

What followed was a stunning display of color, a gradual progression to pink, then a softening to warm orange and gold. This amazing light whose source lay far beyond the horizon chased away the blackness of the night and yet did not in the slightest way diminish the brilliance of the stars. The curled, irregular line to the south became the outline of a towering, cumulonimbus cloud, awash in the same spectacular variegation of red, pink, orange, and gold. An awesome sight.

I realized, then, what it was—this glorious display of changing color. I smiled.

This was no extraordinary stellar phenomenon. Nothing so rare as the Aurora Australis or the Northern Lights.

It was simply the rising of the moon.

The minutes went by. Before long the picture was complete. The first golden arc of the moon broke the horizon and then, full and round, it climbed quickly into the blackness of the night. The more vivid colors gone, its magnificent now-silver glow laced the cloud and filled the eastern sky with a warm luster.

I gazed in awe through the fighter's gunsight and the front panels of the cockpit windshield. This night's moon seemed different. It was not the same familiar "passerby" in the sky. This shining satellite of the earth seemed so close, as if its silken dusty face was to be my landing place. It was a gigantic, round, silver ball, a massive, pockmarked inanimate thing of beauty moving silently, inexorably higher on its journey in space.

Fighter flying is a rather macho business, but this was no macho moment. This was an experience of pure emotion, of pure romance.

Turning down the volume control of the radio I watched in awed silence. To share this moment, so extraordinary and glorious, even with music, was to diminish its splendor.

And, as I gazed, mesmerized at what was before me, a deepening sense of awe and wonder dawned. I was seeing God at work. And he was showing something indescribably beautiful. To me alone. No one else that night on a cloud-enshrouded earth would see what I had seen. I was an audience of one for this amazing demonstration of God's creative genius.

The king and I!

Marvelous words about him from the Psalms burst into my mind. Other verses followed, familiar since childhood but now imbued with fresh and vibrant significance.

> *The heavens declare the glory of God;*
> *the skies proclaim the work of his hands.*

PSALM 19:1

> *When I consider your heavens,*
> *the work of your fingers,*
> *the moon and the stars,*
> *which you have set in place,*
> *what is man that you are mindful of him,*
> *the son of man that you care for him?*

PSALM 8:3–4

There, alone with God, I worshiped him, deeply and emotionally, perhaps in a way I had never done before. I considered the glory of God the Creator. Who was I in the light of that glory? What really is man when he considers the moon and the stars, which God has made?

I had known about God all my life. I had known him—personally, relationally—since teenage years. But at that freeze-moment in time, audience to an astounding demonstration of his glory and creative genius, the wonder of a personal relationship became infinitely more precious. The irony of it all—the smallness, the weakness, the fragility of my humanity, especially as I was squeezed into the restrictive cockpit of a modern-day jet fighter plane. It seemed unspeakable that a connection could ever be made between such a God and myself, yet I knew it was real. He created the connection. He built the bridge—because he loved me. The same power source that brought into being this magnificent silver ball in the sky ahead and placed it in its precise and totally ordered orbit also reached out in love to me and made me his child. He had even said that I could call him "Father."

I couldn't kneel; I couldn't close my eyes. At least not just then. My heart, indeed my very spirit, sang in delightful harmony, at one with God. A solitary jet fighter plane became my strange and beautiful cathedral, the ejection seat my pew. I felt safe there, cradled, held in a security beyond compare.

I belonged to this master painter, this creative genius. He held me firmly, safely, lovingly.

I closed my eyes then, and worshiped. Alone, but not alone.

Now, I reflect with nostalgia on that glorious, stormy night so long ago. And I am reminded of a challenge it held for me. A simple challenge. Clear. Direct.

"Come. Follow me!"

It demanded a response. It still does. ✷

Chapter Two

···Doubts···

> *My son, do not forget my*
> *teaching, but keep my com-*
> *mands in your heart,...Trust*
> *in the LORD with all your*
> *heart and lean not on your*
> *own understanding; in all*
> *your ways acknowledge*
> *him, and he will make*
> *your paths straight.*
>
> PROVERBS 3:1, 5–6

Sometimes we doubt.

It might have been only yesterday when the presence of God seemed so very real. More real, perhaps, than things that were visible. Yet today, from the deep recesses of the mind, something emerges that makes us wonder—and question. The basis of our faith doesn't feel quite as solid as it did before. "What if...?" we ask. Having no ready answers we begin to doubt. And we feel so bad.

It might be an unresolved problem from years ago that should have been long since dealt with. It might be a recurring fear about the future. It might be a flawed relationship that threatens our faith. Our prayers go unanswered. It seems that absolutely nothing can be done about it, and from the depths of our being comes the cry, "Where is God? Where, really, is he?"

It has happened to me on more than one occasion. One of these times was many years ago, when I was still in the military.

I was a proud, young Australian Air Force pilot. My work was exciting, so exciting, in fact, that it didn't feel like work at all. Number 2 Air Trials Unit, based north of Adelaide, South Australia, was a strategic part of an international missile and weapons development strategy. We were embroiled in the cold war. Much of my flying was classified as Top Secret. I was flying seven types of aircraft. Most pilots specialize on one type. No other unit offered anything like this. In the morning I might fly a twin-jet British-built Canberra bomber, testing some aspect of the development of a top-secret missile. In the afternoon I could find myself at the controls of a highly modified fighter, preparing it for its "target" role in the ground to air-missile development program. The next day it might be a bomb ballistics trial in a Vickers Valiant "V" bomber.

In the summer of 1960 we entered the Space Race. I was assigned to work with NASA's Project Mercury. My responsibility was to fly a C-47 "Dakota," specially configured as a test platform to train NASA's tracking crews. My aircraft carried a complete duplicate of the Mercury capsule's instrumentation. Using highly advanced telemetry we could simulate, over Australia's vast, red outback, the passage of a space capsule in orbit.

This was military flying at its best. It could have been said of us, "They have the right stuff."

Many years before, as a teenager, I had promised God that if I were to become a professional pilot I would dedicate my skills and abilities to mission flying whenever and wherever he wanted me to serve. The sense of responsibility to that promise had never left me. Yes, I had a great job. I loved the airplanes I was flying. I loved the people I was working with. It was the fulfillment of my boyhood ambition . . . my dream. But it was only to be for a brief period. I knew that. I had signed on for six years of service and had completed seven. There was always another sort of flying awaiting me . . . somewhere. And so it was with a sense of joyful anticipation that at the peak of my military flying career I submitted the resignation of my Air Force commission.

I will never forget the day in April 1961 when the response arrived. My resignation had been accepted. I would be released from military service on June 30. By this time I had made application and had been accepted by MAF for service as a pilot in New Guinea, conditional upon my release from the Air Force. There was no doubt in my mind that great things were ahead. And yet there was a genuine sadness at the prospect of moving out of my familiar and very much loved world. It was also somewhat threatening to be leaving the financial security of military life, and abandoning a wonderful career, to launch into something about which I really knew so little.

But I had made a commitment. There was no going back. My Air Force career was over. I had burned the bridges behind me.

It was then I began to doubt.

What have you done? I asked myself. *What if it doesn't work out with MAF? What have you got then?* My faith wavered.

Of course it would be okay . . . wouldn't it?

I had been working toward this point for ten years.

Of course God was trustworthy. I had experienced that over and over again. But was he really? Could he be trusted with something as momentous as this?

And as weeks went by, a voice of doubt taunted me, gnawing away at the very basis of my faith.

I became overwhelmed. As the date of release from the Air Force drew nearer, the work I was doing became all the more fascinating and attractive. I became more and more convinced I was a fool to walk away from such opportunity.

My doubt was not restricted to questions about career. It grew deeper. I had always expected that my departure from military life would be like a wonderful graduation. I thought that these would be great days of confidence in God, of joyful assurance that I was walking the right path. Instead I found myself wondering where God was and why he didn't deal directly with my troubled heart and fill me with confident trust. I found myself wondering if I was even right to believe in a "personal call" and if God really did have a plan for my life.

I wondered if he was real at all!

Did it really matter what I did with my life? I was a pilot. Would I not have been much better off to depend on my own ability and take control of my own career?

I told no one of these doubts. I couldn't. I didn't tell my wife. I couldn't tell my Air Force colleagues. My friends at church were even harder to tell. I certainly couldn't tell the MAF people. So I wallowed in my doubts—alone.

MAF had requested that I come to Melbourne for further interviews and orientation. I was very apprehensive about it. Could I hide my doubts from them? Would they see through me? What would they say, or do, if they knew how totally confused I was? Careerwise, MAF was now my only option. If I bombed, where would I be?

Previously I had used an Air Force jet fighter to go to Melbourne. We were required to do a certain amount of "continuation training," and a trip to Melbourne was easily justified as a navigational exercise. This time, though, I decided to drive the 450 miles and stay for the weekend. On Sunday, grasping in my own darkness for a solution to the agonizing dilemma that was taking place within me, I decided to attend a large Melbourne church where a great friend was the pastor. He had been so helpful to me in the past. Perhaps he might have something to say that would rescue me from my terrible despair. I prayed, in the desperation of my doubt, that in his sermons of that weekend there would be a message of reassurance for me.

There was no enlightening message from my pastor friend, no revelation to dispel my gloom. Of course, I was too embarrassed to share my dilemma with him.

I found myself on that Sunday night almost at the end of my ability to cope. I didn't want to talk with anyone. I didn't want to stay in Melbourne. In a very real sense I didn't want to go home either. I was a mess. John Bunyan described my situation so aptly as the "Slough of Despond."

Rather than go back to where I had been staying, I decided to get on the road and drive through the night home to Adelaide.

Having set out soon after the evening church service, I found myself, a couple of hours later, approaching the regional city of Ballarat. Alone in the car, I had cried out repeatedly to the One whom by this time I was almost convinced was a totally disinterested and non-hearing God. With deep emotion, I prayed, "God, what am I going to do? Please help me ... if you are there. I can't go on like this."

There was no answer.

At the western end of Ballarat there is a memorial arch across the highway, a kind of mini "Arc de Triumph." I had passed under this arch many times.

As I approached, traveling at about sixty miles per hour, I noticed a man sitting at its base in the darkness. He stood to his feet and cocked his thumb at me. It was awfully late, about midnight, so I knew he really needed a ride.

I saw the plea in his face as I sped past. *Not tonight,* I thought. *I don't care how desperate you are. I don't want to talk with anyone.* If I had stopped, I could not have hidden from him the emotional upheaval that was taking place in my life. I didn't want to explain this to anyone, let alone a man trying to thumb a lift.

So I drove on.

It must have been thirty minutes later, and at least thirty or forty miles farther along the road, that I began to think a little differently. *Has God ever left me? Was it possible that the voices of doubt, self-pity, and shame were shouting so loudly in my ears that I could not hear what God was saying?*

I had to acknowledge that was not only possible but likely.

Then the thought came to me. Although God hadn't used my friend the pastor to speak to me, there may be others. Suddenly I remembered the stranger standing by the arch. Maybe he was there, just for me.

No, that's a ludicrous idea. It's illogical. Ridiculous.

I drove on for a while thinking about him. Who was he? What would he have said to me had I stopped and picked him up? What would I have said to him? No, it was stupid to think that he could be a messenger to me. But slowly the conviction grew in my mind that this man could be of significance to me, that he could have been placed there by God, just for me, at this very moment.

No one saw me stop the car, turn around on the highway, and make my way back toward Ballarat. It was a crazy thing to do. The hitchhiker would, in all probability, be long since gone. But I drove all that way back. I had to do it.

And he was still there.

This time, of course, I was approaching from the opposite direction so he didn't even stand up. He didn't need a ride in the direction my car was headed. I drove through the arch, turned around, rolled down the window, and stopped by him.

"Want a lift?" I asked him.

I guess he couldn't understand why a car should appear out of the darkness from the west, turn around in front of him, and offer him a ride back in a westerly direction. His wariness was apparent. "No, thanks. I'm wanting to go back there where you've come from."

"Well, mate, that's where I'm going now. Come on, hop in. I'll take you home."

We didn't say a word to each other for some time as I drove toward Adelaide. I'm sure he was wondering exactly what was happening. I didn't want to talk with him anyway. I just wanted to know if he had something to say—from God!

As I watched him out of the corner of my eye, he sat quietly staring at the dashboard of the car. After a while I noticed a change in his demeanor. He was breathing deeply. I sensed tension, confusion. He sighed a loud sigh, a couple of times, as if something was really bothering him. Then, with a voice filled with emotion, he said to me, "Mate, we haven't talked yet, but I simply have to ask you something. I don't know who you are or why you picked me up. Seems to me you were going the other way. I don't know if you can understand my question, let alone answer it, but I need to ask you something. It's terribly important to me just now."

I didn't want questions from him. I wanted answers! But I told him to go ahead anyway.

"It may seem like a crazy question," he said, "but it's simply this." He hesitated. "Do you believe in God? I have to know."

I was totally startled by what he had said. Who on earth was this man? Driving back to the arch was more an act of desperation on my part than anything else. I was the needy one. From the emptiness of my store of faith I had nothing to offer him. After all, I was the one who stood in need of spiritual help and counsel. How could I, of all people, confirm the reality and presence of God to some stranger, and a hitchhiker at that?

Evasively I said, "Why do you ask a question like that?"

"I'll have to tell you a story," he said. "It'll probably sound ridiculous, but I have to tell you.

"On Saturday I went by train to Melbourne to watch football," he said. "I met some friends there and after the game we went for a quick drink, but it turned out to be anything but quick. My friends and I drank long into the evening, well after the departure time of my train back home. I had no other option but to spend the night there. There's only one train a day on our line on the weekend. So this afternoon I went to the station in plenty of time to catch the Sunday train. And an amazing thing happened there.

"A bloke stood on the footpath preaching. I'm a country boy from Horsham, and street preachers would be a bit of a joke there. But something made me want to listen to him. He described my life exactly. Hopeless. Not a lot of direction. He spoke about God . . . and love. He said that God was the answer to my problems. He told me I could know God like a father. He used the word "lost" . . . exactly how I felt.

"It was time for the train," he continued, "but I couldn't walk away from this man. I had to listen, so I let the train go. What he was talking about was more important than going home."

As my passenger went on with his story, he explained that he had never heard anything like this before. After the street preacher had finished, he had spoken with him personally, asking whether such an amazing story applied to him. And this time, face to face, he heard again the story of God's love, of forgiveness and . . . eternal life. He heard of a savior who died and rose again to draw even football fans to himself.

"I found myself, right there in the street with everybody around, repeating a prayer, the very first prayer of my life. I asked God to forgive me. I asked him to give me that new life I had just heard about," he told me.

"This preacher bloke took me to meet his friends at a church, and speaking with them, I knew that something marvelous had happened to me. I came to Melbourne to watch a footy match and I had found God. Actually, God had found me. Mate, I have never felt anything like the feelings I had there.

"But I had to get home," he said. "I have to be at work in the morning." The people from the church drove me a number of miles out of town to thumb a ride home. It was quite a while before anyone stopped for me. I got as far as Ballarat a couple of hours ago. I've been sitting under that arch for ages trying to get another ride.

"I gotta admit. Last night was amazing, but sitting there alone in the cold has been a bad, bad time. I've been turning over in my mind all that happened in Melbourne.

"But then I began to doubt.

"What really had happened? Could my life have been so totally changed through hearing a story and praying a prayer? Who were those people? How do I know it's true? None of my family or friends believe this stuff. How am I going to tell them? Have I been hoodwinked or brainwashed by some religious nut?

"So, I've been sitting at the base of that arch arguing with myself and asking God to show himself to me. I'd almost decided to forget the whole thing. Maybe it was something weird that had happened and that should be forgotten. But I couldn't do it. It had been too real."

He went on with his incredible story as the miles passed by.

"Finally," he said, "just before you came, in desperation I stood and cried out to God the second prayer of my life. 'If you are real, God, please send someone to tell me. Please. Please.'"

He looked across at me, pleading. "So, do you think this is all crazy, or not? Whether you can answer my question or not, I have to ask it. Do you believe in God?"

Did I believe in God? This newborn believer, fresh in the knowledge of a salvation that was real but already under threat, was asking me to confirm the validity of his actions in Melbourne the previous evening. As his story unfolded, I had heard the voice of God speaking to me, answering the cries of my own soul, filling me with a new certainty of faith. This was a divine appointment—for me! I was totally reassured. My reassured heart said to me, "Go on, you tell him. Tell him that God is real. Tell him that God is utterly and completely trustworthy."

And so I did.

"You've told me your story," I then said to him. "Now I have to tell you mine. Yes, God is trustworthy. God is real. Even in the times of heart-wrenching doubts. In fact, he is here in this car. Right now. My doubts, your doubts, don't change him at all. And I've been brought here to tell you just that. He does love you. He is love. And last night he gave to you the honor of knowing him personally."

I went on to share with him my own terrible time of doubting. I told him of my need for someone to come into my life and bring me God's message of assurance. I told him that I believed he was that person. God had sent him to me. . . .

A great and wonderful encounter took place in the middle of that cold Australian night in a yellow Holden car. The Creator of the universe poured out blessing into that car upon two very needy young men. He took a brand-new-baby believer and through him lifted me out of the depth of my misery and despond, never to doubt his reality again. And he took me, in my wretched state of personal need, and through me lifted a new but wavering child-in-the-faith, to nurture him and set his feet on the right path.

It blows my mind to think of God working so intricately and beautifully with his children. He tells us that he is a shepherd, tenderly caring for his flock, giving special attention to the newborn and to those who wander away.

I thought I could unravel the tangled mess of my life myself. I wanted to be alone that night in my car, wallowing in confusion and misery. But God had a better way. He knew that what I really needed was to be reminded that he, God, remains essentially relational. He works through people. Even the youngest of his children.

And he never stops loving us, even when we doubt him the most. ✷

Chapter Three

··· Two Small Sticks ···

May I never boast except in the cross of our Lord Jesus Christ.

GALATIANS 6:14

*L*ike so many other thousands of the people of Papua New Guinea, the people of Lake Kuvanmas had no outside contact. They lived in total isolation.

I had flown over Kuvanmas hundreds of times. A beautiful, deep, black-water lake nestling in the foothills on the northern side of the ranges, it had often been a welcome navigational fix after long periods of flying above the clouds.

Many times, on a routine flight into the mountains I had looked down at a village by the lake and wondered about its people. What were they like? What did they make of my noisy airplane, a speck in the sky above? What were their beliefs and customs?

Our first contact with the people of Kuvanmas came midmorning of a tranquil day, with the bright sun high in the sky overhead. Landing a floatplane there offered no operational obstacles. The lake was long and broad.

The people there welcomed us with warmth. After showing us around their village they invited us into their homes. I had to almost get down onto my hands and knees to enter the doorway of the house to which I was taken.

It was round, about forty feet in diameter. The walls were made of split tree trunks about ten inches wide, tied together with jungle vine. Thatched grass formed the conical shaped roof, bare earth the floor.

Inside, the house was very dark, and initially I could see nothing but the red embers of cooking fires smoldering in the center of the single room. Thin shafts of light from holes in the roof pierced the smoke-filled air creating parallel streaks of gray-white in the darkness. Chinks of light also shone from spaces between the timbers of the walls. In time I could make out woven food bags, fishing nets, and other equipment hanging from the roof. Bows and arrows leaned against the wall by the door. Blackened clay cooking pots and other household utensils were stacked close to the fire.

Slowly, as my eyes became accustomed to the darkness, I began to make out the grinning smiles of mummified human corpses, like a silent macabre audience, seated, with folded arms and crossed legs, around the walls of the house.

Emerging from the darkness, a boy, about twelve, came forward. He placed something in my hand. It was heavy. It felt like a stone, but I couldn't see it clearly. I shifted forward to catch a shaft of light on my hand. It was indeed a stone, a round, smooth piece of granite. But carved deeply into the surface of this stone, as if by some ancient hand, was the figure of a strange, semihuman face.

I had seen such things before, but only rarely. To these people, carved stones like this were sacred things. They represented the spirits of their ancestors and were never shown to outsiders.

"What's the significance of this stone," I asked, "and why are you showing it to me?"

"It's a spirit stone," he replied, stumbling with the unfamiliar pidgin language we were using. "This stone is the spirit of my *tumbunas* . . . my ancestors."

I asked him how it was that he, a young boy, came to possess such a thing, let alone show it to me. They were usually only in the care of family elders or those who had a special spiritual role among the people. They were never the playthings of children. He explained to me that his father and uncles were all dead and so the guardianship of this sacred stone had been passed down to him.

"But now . . . I no fear. I know other spirit God. He is true. He . . . strong!" he added confidently in his broken pidgin English.

Then he retreated into the darkness. I wondered what he would bring back to me this time. Returning, he placed something else in my hand. Sticks? Moving again to the same shaft of light, I was astonished to see what he had brought to me.

Two small sticks were crudely tied together to form a cross.

"This isn't from the time of your *tumbunas,*" I exclaimed to him. "It's just two sticks tied together."

Now, more animated, he proceeded to tell me in an excited way about the life of Jesus! He told me of healing and other miracles. He told me that the wooden cross had to do with Jesus' death, that it was on something like this that he died.

Trying to ascertain the extent of his understanding, I asked him why anyone, let alone a god, would allow men to kill him when he had the power to escape death. He explained that this was not an ordinary man. He was God. He was not a spirit who lives in a carved stone. He can't be defeated or overcome by the power of another family's spirit. And he had to die. He died for the people who killed him. Then he added, "He died for me."

I could hardly believe what I was hearing. God was already there at Kuvanmas in the life of this young boy!

As I asked him more about the life and death of Jesus, he was able to answer, simply but confidently. His belief and faith in God were remarkable.

This was a primitive, untouched place. These were people of an ancient culture. To this boy, my world of relative sophistication was entirely unknown. Yet we shared an astounding commonality across a broad cultural gap. We were poles apart in background, in age, and experience. But in that unforgettable meeting, God brought together two of his children who shared a great treasure.

I told him that I too knew the same story of Jesus, that he was my God as well.

"What missionary told you about Jesus?" I inquired. But he didn't even know the word *missionary!* Or the word *pastor,* or *evangelist.* He certainly didn't have a Bible. There had been no presentation of the Good

News at Kuvanmas. I was amazed. "How did you hear?" I asked him. "Who told you?" His response, his story, was amazing.

He told me something of the culture of his people and explained their system of trade. Certain periods of the year were allocated for barter between the tribal groups. Territorial barriers, normally crossed only at the threat of death, were opened and free travel was allowed.

The Kuvanmas people, for instance, had an abundance of meat. They hunted in the surrounding forests and dried and cured meat in village smokehouses. But they had no clay to make cooking pots. They lacked other essentials as well. So as the time of open trade approached, they stockpiled their smoke-dried meat and then took it many miles through the forest and across vast wetland areas to the Sepik River. There the people had plenty of fish but very little red meat. They also had plenty of clay in their homeland, so the Sepik people exchanged with the people of Kuvanmas clay cooking pots for dried red meat.

My new friend told me of his traveling with the trading party, day after day, through the swamps and down the rivers until they reached the faraway Sepik River village where the exchange of goods traditionally took place. What an adventure for a young man!

The bartering sessions were carried out with great seriousness and complex ritual. Young boys were not allowed to attend; consequently he was forced to wait outside in that strange, unfamiliar, even hostile village.

"The ceremonies went on for three days," he explained. "I made friends with a Sepik boy about my own age. We talked much. We sat by the river and in his house. And we walked through his village, talking together. He told me the story of Jesus. He told me about this one who is truly God. We talked of almost nothing else. It was there I believed. It was there we made this cross."

The grinning, mummified faces and the parallel shafts of light in the dark, smoky air added impact to the telling. What a marvelous story of God's love, reaching into the most unexpected places. Just as the sun shone a ray of light through the roof above me, so God's love had shone into the heart of one young boy through the life and faith of another.

Just two sticks! ✷

Chapter Four

··· Why? ···

> *I will speak out in the*
> *anguish of my spirit,*
> *I will complain in the*
> *bitterness of my soul. . . .*
> *I prefer strangling and death,*
> *rather than this body of mine.*
> *I despise my life; I would not*
> *live forever. Let me alone; my*
> *days have no meaning.*
>
> JOB 7:11, 15–16

"Oh God, please. Make her stop."

My prayer was born out of startled shock as I stood with a group of men encircling the bent-over, blood-stained figure of a Papua New Guinean woman.

But God didn't make her stop. And I couldn't.

As soon as I moved forward to intervene, my arms were gripped by two of the men standing alongside me. Their fingers bit deeply into my flesh. Their scowling faces and words of unmistakable rebuke made it abundantly clear that I was to do nothing. I wasn't wanted there. This was their culture. They wanted me to leave.

The woman was killing herself, and I could do nothing about it.

It was gruesome, abhorrent, and shocking. The beliefs and practices of these mountain people, the men restraining me, demanded that I did not interfere. I did not understand this rare and violent clash of cultures. They were in control.

The place was a small airstrip at Lake Kopiago in the western highlands of Papua New Guinea. It was about noon on a clear bright day in 1965, and I had flown to Kopiago to deliver a load of freight to the mission staff there. Usually a small crowd stood around the parking bay when the airplane arrived. This time there was no crowd. And the young national man from the mission who always came to meet me was nowhere to be seen. Something was wrong. He was always on time.

But he was there. As I shut down the engine, he appeared, running over to the plane from a short distance away where a group of about twenty men were gathered. Whatever was happening there, they were intently involved.

My friend was deeply disturbed and pulled me by the arm toward this group as soon as I stepped down from the plane. "Please come. Maybe you can help," he said as he hurried me over toward the group. "They won't let me do anything to stop her." He forced a way for me through the men to the center of the circle.

I could hardly believe what I saw next.

A Kopiago lady was kneeling on the ground. Her head and body were covered in blood. It ran in rivulets down her face, congealing on her bare body, her thighs, and her knees. Spattered blood covered the gray stony ground on which she knelt. In her bloodied hands she clutched a large, round river stone. She was beating her own head to a bloody pulp. Her forehead was completely split open.

The men stood around in silence, watching but not interfering.

Again she lifted the stone from between her knees with both hands and with what seemed superhuman force smashed it into her forehead. The stone fell to the ground, and her head dropped to her knees as she reeled in semiconscious agony. Forcing herself back into consciousness a minute or so later she picked up the bloodied stone and did it again. Over and over she repeated the horrendous self-inflicted hammering. I couldn't believe her strength and the force she was able to generate. I couldn't believe that she could survive what she was doing to herself. It was as if she were controlled by some external power.

Within minutes she lay face down on the blood-spattered rocks, unconscious again and, I thought, dying. I struggled to be free, to help her. But I was held fast by the men and was unable to move. After watching for a while, I finally pulled myself free and turned away with a sickened heart. I could do nothing.

The men were glad to see me go. They were angry with me for trying to interfere. I was angry with them for not allowing me to do so.
They said very little. Only that the woman had lost a child earlier that
morning. Her one remaining child. She had called upon the tribal spirits of the Kopiago people to save her child, but to no avail. She had previously lost her husband, and now all of her children. Grief and anguish
drove her to this gruesome action. Life held no hope for her. It was not
worth living.

A short while later, as I took off from Kopiago, I could see the small
group of men still encircling that dreadful scene. Yet, the next time I
landed there I was greeted with the usual friendly smiles. There was no
mention of what had happened previously. It was something I knew I
could never understand. It was an incident that had come and gone.

But Kopiago for me is always synonymous with pain. And deep,
spiritual need.

Why bother with mission?

I face the question often these days.

In some circles these days the word *missionary* seems to carry connotations of yesteryear. "Mission belongs to another generation," they
say. Many times I have been asked why I have spent my life helping missionaries in cross-cultural situations. "You people in mission are over-
bearing and patronizing. You will achieve nothing other than the
destruction of wonderful tribal cultures."

I could take those people, with their criticisms, to remote and exotic
places all over the world and show them what has been done in the
name of Christian mission.

I could show them people whose culture remains intact. I could
show them hospitals, medical facilities, and flying doctor services that
bring relief from the hopelessness of former days.

Mostly, I'd like to show them Kopiago. God has done a great work
of grace among the people of the Lake Kopiago area since those early

days of mission. Once, in an earlier time, suicide was the only answer to the agony of a lonely woman's quiet grief, and the hopelessness of life. In the lives of so many of them, despair has been replaced by hope! The people of Kopiago are now permeated by the knowledge, the powerful presence, and the real comfort of God who created them and loves them.

Why? Why interfere with these people? Why bother with missions? For me, the answer lies at the cross of Christ.

And amongst the stones of Kopiago. ☆

PART
TWO

Chapter Five

···Hope on a River's Edge···

And hope does not disappoint us, because God has poured out his love into our hearts by the Holy Spirit, whom he has given us.

ROMANS 5:5

"Can we really land down there?" A muddy river snaked its way through heavily timbered slopes, which rose magnificently on both sides. I made a low run to measure the length of water available. The river ran fast. I could get down. Easily. The judgment call was whether I could get off again. Another timed, low-level run along the river gave me the confidence I needed. There were no rocks or swirling whirlpools, no tree trunks protruding from the river bank. The length of available water was okay.

This was flying at the ragged edge. There was no control tower, no support system, no one to help if anything went wrong. Only a narrow, murky river winding its way through a steamy jungle plateau in the mountains.

This was flying at its best. This was what I loved! Untidy as is! The Air Force had offered nothing like this!

As the keel of the floats kissed the surface of the river with the familiar "hiss," we had no way of knowing what we were about to confront.

The floats settled deeper into the water. Moments later, we sat midriver, the little plane dwarfed by a huge, overhanging canopy of trees. Tresses of drooping vines formed giant curtains of green, screening an ancient and pristine forest.

The eastern reaches of the Erave River in Papua New Guinea seemed a century away from anywhere.

But just seventy miles away lay Kapuna, where the story begins.

Like many other Papuan villages, Kapuna wasn't a particularly pleasant place to live. Every day heat and humidity hovered together around the high nineties. The nights brought little respite. Remote and primitive, it was hardly a place for two brilliant doctors.

But Peter and Lyn Calvert were not ordinary people.

These "Delta Doctors" had raised their children there, in Kapuna. Their house, constructed mainly of crude materials cut from the surrounding bush, looked much the same as all the other village houses. It stood perched on large log stilts high above the ground to keep it clear of the water that at high tide often inundated the entire village. Their furniture was of rough-hewn jungle wood. Fine nets draped over each bed, providing the only protection from malaria-carrying mosquitoes. But mosquito nets captured the heat and made the nights all the more oppressive.

The hospital, also built mainly with material from the surrounding jungle, was the essence of simplicity.

But the medical service the Calverts provided was of the highest order. It came with few of the trappings of the sophisticated hospitals in which they had trained and served. But there, in Kapuna, they conducted a nursing school, sharing their knowledge with scores of young women and men who came from villages hundreds of miles away to be educated in medical practices.

And from that unique little place the Calverts reached out. The people of every isolated village, every hamlet along the hundreds of miles of rivers and steamy swamps became the object of their devotion. Their transportation was as basic as the environment in which they worked. No smart luxury vehicles. No trappings of success. In long wooden canoes hacked from jungle logs, they spent tedious hours, sitting at the stern, a hand wrapped around the throttle of an outboard motor. From village to village they traveled, delivering babies, dispensing medications, binding wounds, suturing gashes, diagnosing and treating all manner of disease and sickness.

Their children, in turn, also spent many hours in those canoes, schooled en route in correspondence lessons by Mom or Dad.

Though remote and isolated, Peter and Lyn were known by their voices all across the country. Each day they conducted a noon-hour medical clinic by high-frequency radio transceiver. Sometimes barely discernable above the scrambled static, diagnoses were made and treatment recommendations given. And on stations hundreds of miles away, mission nurses and medical workers strained to hear. No one could have been more respected and loved by so many. But they never met the Calverts, other than on the radio.

MAF longed to help them. We were able to offer our service and support to hundreds of other mission medical staffs around the country. But not to those at Kapuna. Not to the Calverts. There was no dry land there to make into an airstrip, even the few hundred yards required for our Cessnas. The whole region was one vast expanse of rivers and swamps.

But in 1967, our dream became a reality. We decided to remove the undercarriage from one of our Cessna 180 land planes and fit the airplane with floats. This gave us access to many areas where airstrips were impossible to build. New people were reached, new areas opened.

Kapuna, in the hot and steamy Papuan Gulf, was accessible.

And so a new era of medical work began at Kapuna. Nursing teams came from surrounding regions. Graduates of the nursing school came back for concentrated periods. The floatplane would fly teams from one village to another—an airborne shuttle-service of compassion and care.

Quickly, the value of our service became apparent. Utilizing our aircraft, the Calverts could cover the major part of an entire year's village visitation schedule in eight days of concentrated work. Time formerly consumed by such slow, tedious travel could now be spent in more productive work.

It was just a year or so later that Peter Calvert, who was always on the lookout for some means to extend the limits of his extraordinary work, began talking about exploring new areas. He talked of people who lived far away to the north—in places never before reached by white men.

I had thought that the area he had in mind was uninhabited. It was a wild, forgotten area, densely timbered. A series of huge waterfalls and raging rapids made river contact from the swampy flatlands of the coastal belt impossible. There was a heavy population in the highland valleys away to the west and the north. But this was "half-way" territory. It was "no man's land."

Peter insisted that we fly there to take a look. And he was not easily put off.

Having removed the back seats and all unnecessary weight from the aircraft to lighten it as much as possible, the two of us took off on this new adventure. Peter read the map excitedly, looking along the way for any evidence of humanity. Privately I was thinking to myself that the journey would be a waste of time.

To the west the river roared in a torrent. The airplane couldn't land there. To the east there were many waterfalls and rapids. I couldn't land there. But on this high plateau near some smaller mountains, I could land. And there were, indeed, people. Their small hamlets were clearly visible from the air.

Peter was right.

Having gingerly set the airplane down on the water, we felt a sense of excitement.

The men of the village, all naked, peered at us. There were no women to be seen. No children. We assumed from past experience that they were hidden in the surrounding jungle, frightened by this huge, noisy bird.

These tough highland warriors waved their menacing spears, bows and arrows, and heavy clubs.

We taxied past the first group. They ran through the jungle to augment the group that waited around the bend at the second group of houses. As we continued by, they too ran off through the jungle to augment the next group. Rounding the last bend of this quiet section of the river, we saw a hundred or so men waiting.

We hoped it was a friendly greeting party.

I shut down the engine and steered the airplane to the muddy shore. After securing it firmly we climbed the bank with uncertain smiles. This was scary. But the men appeared to be as apprehensive as we were.

With weapons in hand they surrounded us. One stepped forward slowly and tentatively. He touched our skin, then began feeling our bodies all over!

It was a meeting of two worlds. A young man stood leaning on a crudely fashioned crutch. Wrapped around his leg was a matted mess of grass and leaves. "He probably has nothing more than an untreated tropical ulcer," Peter explained to me. Then opening his medical bag and kneeling on the ground beside the man, he gently cut away the primitive bandage. The leg was swollen and inflamed. The wound was red, but tinged with gray, putrid, rotting flesh.

The man grimaced, then cried out in pain. Shouts of strong rebuke accompanied the slapping noise of arrows being placed at the ready.

"Leave him alone."

But Peter kept working slowly, carefully. He filled a shiny kidney-shaped dish with sterile water and tenderly washed that horrible sore. The man moaned, trying to be strong. I watched in silence. The tension was almost palpable.

But Peter's tenderness was obvious. The arrows, one by one, were put away. Soon these jungle warriors were squatting on their haunches around us, a sure demonstration that they no longer felt threatened.

Heads began to nod. There was whispered conversation. They had never seen compassion from a stranger.

Having cleansed the wound, Peter used an atomizer to puff sulfur powder into it. He gave the boy an injection of antibiotic. Gasps of amazement came from the men as he bound the leg with a pure white bandage.

The work was done. A bridge . . . of compassion . . . had been built. Friendship was established.

We showed them our airplane and toured their village, catching sight of an occasional female face staring from the jungle.

Words weren't possible, but we explained to them that we would return in a month. We drew pictures in the sand with a stick. Thirty lines, one for each day in the lunar cycle. We scratched pictures of the phases of the moon between those lines, and then, pointing to the crescent moon in the blue sky, we told them that we would come back when the moon was once again in its present setting. They understood.

By the time we climbed aboard our little Cessna, we were like old and treasured friends. As we sped by on the takeoff run, they were waving excitedly. We were soon on our way back to Kapuna.

What a day it had been.

And one month later, to the day, with the crescent moon against the blue sky, Peter and I returned.

To our astonishment, the village had been totally transformed. Women and children were there with the men at our landing place. Bodies glistened with fat and tree oil; heads and arms were adorned with feathers and crimson and yellow flowers. These new friends of ours yelled and waved their welcome. Women lined a path from the river bank to the center of the village where the older men awaited us. We felt like VIPs inspecting a military guard of honor as we walked between the rows of excited, laughing women.

Every house in the village was decorated with the same crimson and yellow flowers. The assembled elders greeted us ceremoniously. They led us, with great pride, to a brand-new house they had built for us!

Into "our" new home they brought the sick and the wounded. Men and women, the young and the old. And Peter cared for them there.

Our former patient needed no further treatment. His leg had healed. He stood watching, almost preening, without his crutch. His was a joyful pride.

At noon they had a feast prepared for us, a delicious meal of chicken cooked in coconut cream. It was worthy of inclusion on the menu of any five-star restaurant.

We saw no fear. There was none of the apprehension of the previous month. Instead we saw excitement. Most of all, we saw hope!

A month earlier, with primitive and awkward gestures, we had said that we would come back. But did they believe it? Would they just sit and talk about it? And hope? Or would they do something in preparation for our return?

They had decided to put their hope into action. It was apparent. They had planned for the day we would return. They had worked hard throughout that month in preparation. They had decorated their village *with hope!*

Hope built that house for us. Hope did the cleaning. Hope gathered the flowers. Hope prepared the feast.

In their limited understanding they only saw that what we brought was physical healing. Their hope was that this would continue. And it did.

Yet the day was coming when they were to see the miracle of a deeper hope. The hope of spiritual healing. And, in time, they received that hope as well. Faith in God through Jesus.

"Our" home became the home of their first pastor. For a time it was also their church. And many of those people became evangelists, carriers of the hope they had found, to others in that remote area.

And that is another wonderful story. ✯

Chapter Six

···Triumph and Tragedy··· at Tifalmin

The light shines in the dark-
ness, but the darkness has
not understood it. . . .
The true light that gives
light to every man was
coming into the world. . . .
To all who received him, to
those who believed in his
name, he gave the right to
become children of God—
children born not of natural
descent, nor of human
decision or a husband's will,
but born of God.

JOHN 1:5, 9, 12–13

Tifalmin was breathtakingly beautiful.

The rugged peaks to the west reaching up to fourteen thousand feet were
often lost in billowing clouds. The
mountains to the north and to the
south, though no less rugged, lowered
progressively to seven thousand feet to
the eastern end of the valley. The river,
which curled its way eastward through
the valley, was the run-off of almost daily
storms that drenched the mountains.
The river finally threw itself over a
waterfall, filling the air with a misty
spray.

From above, the valley seemed a
place of peace. Smoke of a hundred cooking fires rose lazily above the
trees, softening the tranquil scene with a blue-gray haze.

The airstrip at Tifalmin had been cut from timbered land alongside
the river in the center of the valley. For the many hands, thousands of
hands, it had not been light work. Barely five hundred yards long, with
rising ground at the western end, the airstrip left no room for error. One
learned to place the airplane's wheels on the stony ground right at the

airstrip's threshold. It was a one-way airstrip. There was no "go-around," no second chance.

The Cessna seemed so delicate and fragile against the towering mountains. It was a hostile environment for flying. The upward thrust of warm tropical air forced aloft by the rugged terrain could bring rapid change to weather conditions. Flying here called for more than the normal vigilance.

Tifalmin was no place for a Saturday afternoon recreational pilot.

But Tifalmin is most memorable for me not because of its unique beauty or because of the challenge of landing an airplane there. Tifalmin is memorable because of its people, memorable because in that valley I would witness the triumph of God. But, as well, people I knew and loved would pay the greatest of all human sacrifice.

The piercing, challenging, unflinching stares from the men were my first impression of these people. Their eyes, with a peculiar redness, perhaps the result of living in smoke-filled houses, issued a clear warning. This environment belonged to them. It was their valley, their world. They were the masters. Little covered their nakedness. Long gourds, secured with a thin woven cord around the waist like athletic straps, rather than cover their nakedness seemed only to accentuate it!

Most of them wore two black feather quills inserted into holes punctured in the side of each nostril. These quills crossed in the center of their foreheads. Many had whitened bones or a large pig's tooth inserted horizontally through the stretched septum of the nose. The biceps of some of the men were wound with what seemed like blackened and withered sinews, the sex organs of wild boars. They were the mark of the great hunter and were worn with pride.

There was no shame, no coyness about these men. Only pride.

The weapons they carried also created an immediate impression. Black palm bows were strung with cane bowstring capable of taking as much tension as those strong, muscled arms could produce. Arrows designed for a variety of targets were carried, always at the ready. Some arrows, tipped with hard, black palm wood and finely sharpened bone, were intricately carved and painted with rich brown ochre.

These were for the killing of men.

The women were different. Their clothing was skimpy, just a thick grass skirt no more than six inches in length hanging in front, below the waist. Some wore a similar skirt at the back. Even so, this brief covering seemed more modest than that of the men. And the ladies of Tifalmin were coy, shy, lowering their heads and turning away upon eye contact with strangers.

The women were the workers, the gardeners of the community. They bore the evidence of this special role. Their hands were cracked and gnarled, their bodies well-encrusted with the rich volcanic earth of that remarkably fertile place.

Children were everywhere. Dirty babies suckled dirty breasts. A baby not suckling was carried in a woven string bag suspended from the forehead and hanging down the back of its mother. Other bags, similarly slung over the head, contained food and other household necessities. Older children, carried on the hips of their mothers, gnawed on pieces of sweet potato.

The women of Tifalmin were tough. They did the hard physical work.

The houses were well constructed of material from the surrounding bush. Round, with only one room, they were double walled of woven, beaten bamboo. The densely thatched grass roof entrapped smoke from the permanent fire inside and allowed it to escape only in lazy, fine wisps which to the unfamiliar gave, from the outside, the impression that the house was slowly smoldering away.

It was the women who took most of our attention on the first day I visited Tifalmin. It was "mothers-and-babies" day. And two of my passengers were nurses who came here regularly to conduct an infant-welfare clinic. My other passenger was a male missionary, faced with the long-range challenge of creating relationships with the men.

There was a lot of chatter as the day got underway. The old-fashioned, round-faced scale that was hung over a low branch of a nearby tree seemed more designed for weighing garden produce than babies. A portable table was erected upon which the tools of the nurse's trade were laid out ... stethoscope, auriscope, forceps, syringes, scissors, and so forth.

Despite much protesting and noisy howling, each baby was weighed. The auriscope was used to check the babies' ears. There was a careful feeling of the spleen for any swelling or tenderness in that area, a certain indication of malaria. Each mother was questioned closely about feeding and other important indicators of good mother/baby care. Some babies were given injections, always to the familiar cries of protest.

Ear infections were rampant among children at Tifalmin. With each family living in a one-roomed house, a baby's crying was often the cause of domestic tension, so the Tifalmin women would take a small beetle, which, when placed in the ear of a crying baby, could be guided to crawl down into the aural canal. Its movement would bring soothing relief, albeit temporarily, to the baby. I have watched on a number of occasions as those nurses, with great care, removed a rotten gray mess of dead beetles from a little baby's ear.

Infant mortality brought its own special anguish to the mothers of Tifalmin.

Our activity on one end of the parking bay was "women's stuff." The men, armed and dangerous-looking, sat around small fires on the other end. There was little talk. They were not relaxed. Their bows and wicked-looking arrows were held close, always at the ready. Treachery was the mark of stature among the men. Fear kept their horizons small and defenses strong. Life was cheap, often snatched away by sickness and infection about which they knew so little. Or by enemy tribes.

They listened attentively, nevertheless, to the missionary's stories about creation, about heaven and earth, about God. They themselves were also great storytelling people. But while the women were literally pouring out their love and gratitude for the care they were receiving, the men, still with their weapons close at hand, remained serious, unsmiling. We had invaded their territory.

At the end of the day they stood still and gazed intently as my passengers squeezed back into the plane for the return to Telefomin. It was a short flight, only five minutes, and hardly worth an entry in a logbook. But it had nevertheless been a flight spanning a thousand years, a flight into the Stone Age.

When I flew back to Wewak, I said to Jo, "The medical work is amazing. And so deeply appreciated. But the teaching, the mission work—that's a different matter. It will take generations before a result is seen."

We were in the business of bringing the light to Tifalmin, but as Scripture says, "The darkness did not understand it."

Two years later, on a Sunday morning, I stood again by that same beautiful river at Tifalmin. Many hundreds of the villagers had gathered there. They looked the same, wore exactly the same scant clothing. But by this time something was different.

There were no scrutinizing and distrusting stares. No challenging, piercing eyes demanding that we look away. And as a greater contrast—there were no bows, no arrows, no clubs. There were no weapons at all.

I waded into the crystal-clear, cold water to sit on a rock a few yards from the shore, and somewhere, someone began to sing. It was nothing familiar, and not in a melodic form familiar to my Western ear. A strange tribal chant. But it was a rich and beautiful song that gladdened the heart of God. Then, as the singing continued, one by one, thirty or so of those Tifalmin people, women and men, waded out into that river pool to be baptized.

The valley looked the same. The same gray-blue smoke rose lazily to paint the valley with early morning haze. The mountains still rose from the east with their black western peaks disappearing into billowing masses of cloud. The same sparkling river wended its way through the valley to throw itself in a mass of spray over that last rock face.

But Tifalmin was not the same. The corner of a heavy blanket of fear and darkness had been lifted. The light had come. It had penetrated that beautiful little valley and had begun to make things new!

Later that afternoon I sat in my aircraft, the engine already started, running down the pretakeoff checklist. Through the whirling blades of the propeller I could see a group of Tifalmin people. I could see the loving smiles of the women and the laughing grins of those mountain warriors—my friends.

It seemed as if I could hear a clear, resonating voice from above the clouds that were beginning to fill the valley, an almost audible benediction.

"You are a chosen people, a royal priesthood, a holy nation, a people belonging to God, that you may declare the praises of him who called you out of darkness into his marvelous light."

Walt and Vonnie Steinkraus, translators with Wycliffe Bible Translators, died at Tifalmin village in 1971. With their three children!

The Steinkrauses had come from America to live at Tifalmin as the church came to life. From the air their house was hardly discernible from all the other village houses. Its only distinguishable feature was two lengths of corrugated iron sheeting laid on the roof to catch rain water and channel it into two fifty-gallon drums that stood outside the house.

Walt and Vonnie went without modern conveniences. They lived simply, identifying as much as possible with the lifestyle of the people. Skilled in linguistics, they were committed to the long and arduous task of reducing the hitherto unrecorded language to print and then to the even more challenging task of translating into that language the Word of God.

Vonnie Steinkraus grew roses at Tifalmin. The fertile soil of that highland valley responded well to her green fingers, and on a number of occasions I flew away across the mountains toward home carefully sheltering a single cut rose under the pilot's seat. A rose was a treasure for Jo in humid, tropical Wewak.

Tifalmin was a lonely place for the Steinkraus family. It was far from the ordinary. But Walt and Vonnie Steinkraus were not ordinary people. The Steinkrauses had long-range plans.

Sunday was always a nonflying day for MAF, but we made ourselves available for emergency flights. Early on a Sunday morning one of the staff would receive and deal with any requests received on the HF radio. Usually these would be medical emergencies only.

On this particular Sunday a radio message came from Telefomin. It was a strange message: "There are calls of anguish and distress being shouted from village to village saying that something very serious has happened at Tifalmin. Could you please come to fly us over there?"

Within minutes I was on my way, climbing toward the dark, rugged peaks ahead. Upon arrival at Telefomin, the turn-around was rapid, and I was soon headed toward Tifalmin with friends from the Baptist Mission as my passengers.

The valley presented its usual tranquil, smoky calm. It wasn't until we flew over the airstrip that we saw it.

It was a stark evidence of a horrible disaster. Across the valley, on the other side of the river opposite the village, thousands of tons of sodden earth and rock had fallen away from high ground there. It had somehow been projected outward with such enormous force that it had literally rained down from above, onto the village of Tifalmin.

Tifalmin village no longer existed.

In its place were acres of brown, oozing mud about twenty feet thick. Thousands of protruding tree trunks, like snapped limbs, punctured the surface, along with branches, bushes, and rocks. The only houses that had escaped destruction were a few which had been at the periphery of the village. The rest of the village, the church, the school, the Steinkraus house—all were gone, obliterated, crushed, and buried under thousands of tons of mud.

In what remained of the parking bay, a group of Tifalmin people jumped and waved, imploring us to come down to their help.

There was barely enough airstrip for a very short precautionary landing. Half of the airstrip was similarly engulfed in this sodden mess.

I stopped with the aircraft's spinning propeller only feet from a twenty-foot wall of mud.

We were surrounded by a wailing, grieving, sorrowing group of our Tifalmin friends, weeping for their lost village, for their family members whose lives had been taken and who were still buried in that horrible, sodden mass.

Distraught, they wept also for Walt and Vonnie and all three of the Steinkraus children. "They're under there, lost and crushed," they cried.

We slithered and climbed our way to the top of that brown wet hill. For hundreds of yards we could see nothing but thick mud.

"After our time of worship in the church," the people said, "most of us went to secure and cut a large log that was caught in a downstream bend of the river. A few of the older people went back to their houses and did not come. The Steinkrauses went to their house too. Now, all who stayed in the village are lost."

We dug through that mud hour after hour, every day for three days. But our searching was in vain. The thick mass of mud was quickly hardening, impacting in the daytime heat.

It was heart-wrenchingly sad when on the second day we located the body of a beautiful little girl, the youngest of the Steinkraus children. Hers was the only body to be recovered there.

Early on the Sunday morning she had been lovingly dressed for church, all in white. Somehow in death she had been protected from the engulfing mud and rocks by one of the sheets of galvanized iron on the roof. Her little body was barely scratched, hardly dirty in the midst of such filth.

We were a quiet and somber group as we laid her gently back into the mud. It seemed best that she remain there with the rest of her family.

No trace of anyone else was found.

There was only one eyewitness to the disaster, an elderly lady. I was standing by her as she was questioned through an interpreter by a senior government official, one of many people I had shuttled to Tifalmin in the three days following the disaster.

"What did you see?" he asked her.

"I saw the earth falling from the sky upon our home," she replied. "So I ran away down the airstrip, but then I stopped to pray."

"Pray?" came the question. "What on earth did you pray for?"

"I prayed," she said, "that God would take only those who already knew him. I asked him not to allow anyone to die who didn't yet know him. I asked him to take only those who would go to heaven."

This simple mountain woman understood life. She understood death. She understood eternity.

Some years later when I was recounting these events to an Australian friend, he shared with me a wonderful postscript to the Steinkraus story.

As a student my friend John had flown to Papua New Guinea to help in the building of an airstrip in another valley and was working under the direction of Walt Steinkraus. They became close friends. At the completion of their time together, as John was leaving for home,

Walt gave him a signed family photo. The Scripture reference Walt Stienkraus pencilled on the photograph was Psalm 40:2. It says:

> *He lifted me out of the slimy pit,*
>> *out of the mud and the mire;*
> *he set my feet on a rock*
>> *and gave me a firm place to stand.*

Could Walt Steinkraus have had a premonition about his family's death? I don't think so. But from their tomb of mud in the beautiful valley of Tifalmin that Sunday morning, Walt, Vonnie, and their children were lifted, by the Psalmist's God, out of the mud and the mire. Their feet were set upon a rock, and he gave to them a firm place to stand, clean before him.

I saw tragedy at Tifalmin . . . tragedy in human terms. But I saw triumph at Tifalmin . . . triumph in eternal terms.

It is such a little place. It is so insignificant, almost unnoticeable.

But not to God. ✯

Chapter Seven

···The Compassionate Cannibal···

Jesus sent him away, saying, "Return home and tell how much God has done for you."

LUKE 8:38–39

Amusep would climb into the front seat of my Cessna without the slightest hesitation. He was a seasoned traveler—at least in small Cessna aircraft.

Amusep loved to fly!

Perhaps he enjoyed flying so much because he had walked the cloud-enshrouded mountain trails of his homeland since childhood. You only needed to get a glimpse of his bare, callused feet, gnarled and scarred, to know they had carried him over many a rocky ridge and covered countless miles of that brutal mountain country. Perhaps as he gazed down upon the mountain trails from his airborne high vantage point he realized that every minute in the air represented hours of hard, high-altitude mountain trekking.

As a man of the mountains, Amusep was also accustomed to violent weather. He was familiar with the threat of a rapidly developing thunderstorm as it marched across the mountains, filling a highland valley with dense, gray clouds as though poured from a giant, heavenly container.

Which is why, I suppose, it didn't seem to perturb him when one day, shortly after takeoff, billowing dark clouds surrounded the tiny aircraft, and raindrops began snaking their way up the windshield.

Conditions like this worried most other passengers, but not Amusep. This was simply the way we traveled.

He had greater things on his mind.

He was on a mission.

The mark of God was upon Amusep. He knew that his task in life was God-given. He was one of Papua New Guinea's "barefoot evangelists," driven by a strong personal passion. And the airplane? Simply an aid to his task. It projected him into a degree of usefulness that would otherwise have been totally unattainable. To fly across the mountaintops and over the deep valleys at 120 knots when the alternative was a snail-paced, grueling hike was a miracle to him.

This small, slim, but muscular highlander was a man at peace with his Maker. He loved his people and wanted to share this peace with each and every one of them. The isolated villages of the West Sepik region were his parish, the people of those villages the targets of his deep concern.

This was no foreign missionary. Amusep could never be labeled an intrusive outsider. Rather, this was a man who understood. For the culture of the people was his culture too. He knew their fears. He could identify the spirits that lurked in wait for them in the rain forest and stalked them in the dark of night. He grieved over every sickness that so quickly robbed them of life. He understood the things that bound them.

But Amusep was a man who had found freedom. Freedom in Jesus Christ. To him, freedom had not destroyed his culture, but had breathed life into it. Fulfillment and security had replaced anxiety and fear. Light had replaced darkness. Amusep could enjoy the beauty of the night without fear.

He knew the intertribal rivalries and the animosity that created intense pressure. He well knew the "payback" principle that meant no one was safe or secure. He understood the vise grip of evil and treachery that gave little pleasure to the people. And yet he was a man of pleasure, of laughter, and of peace. He had a passion to tell his people that the change had come to him through Jesus.

He knew, also, the heart-wrenching sadness that pervaded the entire society because of the lack of health care. It took an awful toll. The infant mortality rate was a cultural tragedy, and Amusep knew what could be done about it.

To me, Amusep was a tremendous source of information. He taught me about the various tribal groups and of the very firm boundaries between them. He spoke of the response of the people to the message he carried with so much fervor. Though physically just a small man, Amusep was a man of great stature. And while not all were prepared to immediately accept his message, he loved them still. And he always returned to teach more of the Good News he carried.

Because Amusep worked with the Baptist Mission, I had assumed that he had found his faith in Jesus through them. They had recognized his natural leadership ability and trained him well for work in evangelism, health care, and education. He was quite an orator, an excellent interpreter, a marvelous teacher, a persuader of men. . . .

The sky grew dark and threatening as I flew that afternoon. I took off from Telefomin, the center of the Baptist Mission work, to Mianmin, in Amusep's home valley. I was carrying supplies to a team of translators working there and was planning to bring Amusep back to Telefomin. When I landed he greeted me with his familiar grin and, after quickly helping me unload the aircraft, climbed aboard for the return flight. He too had been watching the threatening sky and knew that I would be in a hurry.

Once airborne, we talked about the best way to negotiate our way back through the valleys. There was no chance of outclimbing the rapidly deteriorating weather. We flew west down the Mianmin Valley, trying to find a way under the clouds, following the river into the higher mountains, toward Telefomin. All the while the weather closed in. It was like flying through a tunnel whose floor, heavily timbered, serrated, and rocky, was as threatening as the dark clouds above.

I knew one of the airstrips in the area was available as an alternate. And we could always return to Mianmin. But the thought of spending a wet and cold night there made me persevere just a little bit longer.

There was simply no way through. Black clouds completely filled the valley system ahead and behind. To the left and right, reaching thousands of feet above, clouds were "filled with rocks and trees."

"Roughing it" was going to be the order for the night.

I turned to the left into the narrow entry of another valley, Eliptamin, and soon had the airstrip there in sight. I made a quick circuit and advised the Civil Aviation controller that our intention was to land and stay overnight.

It was beginning to rain by the time my trusty Cessna was parked at the top end.

Amusep was out of the plane in an instant, saying as he darted of into the trees, "Mi painim ples bilong slip bipo ren i cam wasim yumi" ("I'll find a place for us to sleep before the rain comes and drenches us both"). It was raining heavily up toward the Eliptamin village, some distance away. The track was enshrouded with cloud.

The lean-to shelter the mission had built there was soon completely rainproof, thanks to my industrious friend. He had gathered armfuls of a soft fern upon which we would sleep. Marvelous bushman that he was, he very quickly had a large pile of dry firewood safely out of the rain's way and a warm fire burning. I took a few emergency supplies from the airplane while Amusep ventured off into the forest again, returning with some sweet potato that was soon roasting at the edge of the open fire.

The sweet potato looked like charcoal on the outside, but underneath its black crust it was delicious. Huddled in the darkness beneath a crude shelter beside the fire, we enjoyed a great meal. Soon we were lying down, listening to the consistent pattering of the rain on our leafy roof.

Amusep asked me about my earlier life, my home. I told him about my wife and children at Wewak, about my own childhood. I talked of my schooling and my boyhood passion to fly. And I told how I came to Jesus, of the feelings of peace and security that had brought to me.

"What about you?" I asked him. "How did you become a follower of Christ? Was it at Telefomin, through the Baptist missionaries?" He grinned. I think he knew what my reaction was going to be as he told me his story.

"I came to know Jesus when I was in prison," he said.

Prison! He had gotten my attention!

"I was taken to the coast with a number of other men from around here." He gestured with his hand. "We spent ten years locked away there."

In his wonderfully expressive pidgin language he went on, "Some of the other Mianmin men and I killed the first government officers to come into this territory. We ate their bodies. We ate also the bodies of some of their carriers whom we had also killed. But other white men who came searching for their lost friends hunted us. We were caught, taken to court, and sent to prison on the coast. It was in prison, the *kalabus,* that I met Jesus!"

Killed . . . and ate?

I'm sure I swallowed nervously. This man, my gentle friend Amusep, had killed and eaten someone. Someone just like me. And here we were, huddled together. Alone. And I had to spend the night on this dark, isolated mountain airstrip alone with this self-confessed cannibal!

Amusep enjoyed my reaction to his tale.

He told me why that tragedy had taken place. The killing and its horrible aftermath had been motivated not so much out of treachery or maliciousness, but out of fear. The Mianmin people had become increasingly apprehensive. A message had been called from ridge to ridge that a group of strange "spirit figures" had come to the valley to the east and were making their way along the river up toward the Mianmin valley. The members of that early expedition had been totally unaware that their progress along the river valleys was not only being monitored but continually communicated ahead. Thus apprehension among the Mianmin escalated. Day by day their fear grew as these strange creatures came closer and closer.

Perhaps these were the spirits of ancestors coming to wreak some kind of vengeance upon them, they thought. Two of the strangers, it was told, had skins that were not brown but white. And their bodies were covered in a weird, unfamiliar way. Even their feet had some unusual covering.

Fear gripped the people of Mianmin. They had but one alternative. It was well-planned and carefully carried out. These people were masters of ambush. The exploring party had no chance.

That their bodies were ceremonially eaten, simply had to be. It was the fashion—the custom.

There was no pride as Amusep told his story. There was no bitterness about the prison term. Instead, there was gratitude. These primitive mountain men had been taken to the coast and in prison had been taught to read, given simple medical knowledge, mechanical training, and an education in life skills. Thus they eventually returned to Mianmin uniquely equipped to contribute to the development of the area.

But the outstanding memory of his time in prison was of the people, brown and white, who had told him about Jesus.

We marveled together, my friend and I, at the plan of God that had brought us together that night. Two entirely different men, a pilot from Australia and a cannibal-become-pastor from the remote mountains of New Guinea.

Neither of us could fully understand the other's culture. Our languages were different, our homes, our families as well. Amusep certainly had the edge on me in terms of survival skills and bushmanship. But the great central commonality we shared was that each of us had been sought out by God and commissioned to do his work.

The sky cleared, and we prayed together. We were two brothers, worshiping the One who had made the canopy of stars now shining brilliantly above.

I slept well and peacefully that night in the company of this great man from Mianmin. He cared for me so gently, staying awake to tend the fire to keep me warm, watching against any danger that may have lurked there behind us in the forest.

Today, Amusep is in heaven with Jesus. His is a name virtually unknown outside of Papua New Guinea. But he played a significant part in the establishment of a living and vibrant church there in the mountains of Papua New Guinea. And his was a name familiar to the Father of Eternity as he was welcomed into heaven.

We will have a joyful reunion one day, Amusep and I. ✱

Chapter Eight

···No-Nonsense Faithfulness···

Then Jesus came to them and said, "All authority in heaven and on earth has been given to me. Therefore go and make disciples of all nations, baptizing them in the name of the Father and of the Son and of the Holy Spirit, and teaching them to obey everything I have commanded you. And surely I am with you always, to the very end of the age."

MATTHEW 28:18–20

$\mathcal{D}$ick Donaldson was a unique individual.

He invariably looked the same. Same shorts, same short-sleeved shirt, same work boots and socks, and, always, a felt hat. I suppose it was appropriate. But it was always the same.

Dick didn't smile a lot. Except with his eyes, that is.

In those pioneer days of mission work, when the airplane provided the only link to the outside world, warm words of thanks and gestures of appreciation were frequent rewards of the pilot. But not from Dick. "Thanks," he would say. "See you next trip," and he would load a wheelbarrow with supplies we had unloaded from the airplane and wheel it off along the narrow track to the mission house a few hundred yards away.

A taciturn man, Dick would, however, from time to time, involve me in discussion about theological matters. He loaned me a book one day, saying, "Read this, Meyers. It'll do you good. You might not agree with it, but you'll be wrong."

Living where he did, doing what he did, Dick was not internationally known. I could write about any one of the thousands of missionary men and women I have served who have been wonderfully used by God. Dick Donaldson was no "cover story" missionary with a beaming smile.

On the contrary, he was argumentative, aggressive, and tough. He had an air of authority and was confident in what he was doing. He lived out obedience and faithfulness and was prepared to pay the heavy cost of his calling. Without question.

Dick was committed to the Orokana people—and they knew it. The church at Orokana emerged from that primitive society, strong and secure. It had the brush of Donaldson solidarity about it, the same qualities of spiritual life and strength.

We are told that faith can move mountains. Dick Donaldson had moved a mountain. Well, almost! He had built the airstrip at Orokana by moving countless tons of earth. Cutting here, filling there. Every available foot of space on a gently sloping hillside was utilized. Operationally, it was not the easiest of airstrips. It left no margin for pilot error. But it was adequate. And the airstrip was Orokana's lifeline. The Orokana people were the Donaldsons' people. More importantly, the people claimed the Donaldsons as their very own.

Every time I climbed away from Orokana, even after a ten-minute stop, I always had a sense of privilege in being able to serve Dick Donaldson. To me, he was a "father in the faith," a teacher, a role model, even a prophetic voice.

He didn't use many words. But I knew he was appreciative, and his occasional thin smile and wry sense of humor hid a man of joy and rich humor. And in his own unique way, he often gave me the urge to go on to develop and grow.

To Dick the task was urgent and serious. And he always had his sights on even more distant horizons.

The powerful Continental engine droned smoothly on. I made another turn and then another, following a patterned sequence over the vast, unending miles of jungle green. Dick and I were surveying a new area, hitherto untouched. We were sixty miles from Orokana.

With a sheet of paper spread between us, we were talking together, comparing various features visible from either side of the airplane, making our map. We recorded every detail, every feature, traced the flow of every river, compared the position of every ridge. And every village.

Off to the south, dominating the landscape was a huge dormant volcano, Bosavi, rising majestically to over nine thousand feet above the plateau. Although its apex for weeks at a time was lost in thick clouds, Bosavi made a superb reference point.

"Go down to about a thousand feet," Dick said, after a time.

We had drawn our map thus far with the broad strokes of features visible from a higher altitude. Now we had to draw in the finer details. From the lower altitude we could clearly see that each of the "villages" we had observed comprised a few smaller structures surrounding one huge communal dwelling. Each house was built on heavily timbered slopes. Huge vertical logs provided secure protection at the Gout with the family area, an "open porch" at the rear, high above the steeply sloping ground.

By sheer size, each house must have contained many families.

Yet as we flew by, lower again this time, there was not a living soul visible. From one village to another. We knew they were there. Women and children would be well hidden and protected in the surrounding jungle, and the men watching through the trees. The airplane, an unknown creature from far away, with its strange noise, seemed to be searching for them.

It was.

And they hid.

The map had been drawn, the population judgments made; our work was complete. Now the difficult work began. We must find a site for an airstrip.

From the air we had observed that while all around, the timber was heavy and dense, there were cleared areas on the faces of a number of ridges. "Slash and burn" garden sites were under cultivation, and others from previous years were still visible, though swiftly being reclaimed by the voracious forest. It was difficult to see how we could ever land this small Cessna anywhere in that jungle.

Eventually, we chose a sight. It lay in a section of heavily timbered ground, sloping gently upwards along the foothills of Mount Bosavi.

"Now go down low," he said. "Fly over the four largest settlements, very low, very slow." He smiled and had a twinkle in his eye.

"Bring it down," he said. "Ten or twenty feet will do. But make it real slow. I want to have a close look."

I protested, but Dick was undeterred. "Come on, just do it."

So down we went.

Then, as we passed over the first of a number of selected "long houses," Dick, to my astonishment, quickly opened the airplane's window, took something from the rucksack he had on the floor between his legs, and dropped it out the window.

"What on earth are you doing?" I cried. It was hardly an approved action. "What did you throw out the window?"

With that characteristic thin smile, he opened the rucksack and showed me four or five very small cans. It was household paint. To each can he had attached a ribbon.

"It's alright for you," he said. "You can fly from Orokana to Bosavi in twenty-five minutes. It will take me weeks to get out here on foot! And it will be hard enough to see the sun, let alone navigate based upon this crude map we've just drawn. When I get here, how do you think I am going to match map with reality? There has to be a start-off point. I won't even be able to see Bosavi when I'm down there. But I'll tell you what! Those men down there are gonna pick up those cans. They probably already have the first one. I'd be surprised if they aren't already covered in paint. They love the stuff. They'll be the 'red people.'"

So we proceeded, legally or not, merrily dropping cans of paint onto a string of villages. We marked the "red village," the "yellow village," and the "green village," and so on, until his little sack of goodies was completely empty.

That day, a new light began to dawn over the rugged forest area of the Bosavi slopes. And as primitive men felt the oily texture of this strange paint and marked their arms and foreheads . . . and their houses . . . with its rich color, they were unknowingly marked as those who would hear about the greatest outpouring of love that history has ever known.

The noise of the airplane engine, a terrifying thunder to them on that first day, was to become, like an extended drum roll, the prelude to a beautiful symphony of love that would woo them out of darkness into a marvelous light.

The departure of the first Bosavi expedition was something to remember. It had taken many Cessna flights to gather all the people and supplies for this epic trek. There was Dick, same shorts, same short-sleeved shirt, same work boots and socks, same felt hat. Another mission colleague and about thirty or so men from the Orokana area joined him. They carried an incredible quantity of supplies. Metal lockers had been carefully packed. Through each of the long handles of these lockers, wooden poles had been inserted so they could be carried at shoulder height by two men walking the trail in tandem.

As the last of the men disappeared into the heavy jungle with days of arduous mountain travel ahead, I marveled at their courage.

The forest site on the northern slopes of Bosavi slowly, very slowly, took on the appearance of an airstrip. From the air, I could see the criss-crossed trunks of felled trees and a small clearing where Dick's rough camp was established. Within a few weeks it was a gash in the forest, brown among the green. I had said to him, "Prepare a clearing a couple of hundred feet long. Then I'll be able to drop you what you need."

And so the "darkness-to-light" project proceeded. Far away from home and family, alone among new found but primitive friends, Dick worked. He addressed the gargantuan task with vigor. The airstrip was crucial to his plan.

With the airplane's right-hand door removed, it was very noisy. Bags of supplies were balanced precariously on the doorsill as I made the approach low over the tall trees at the upper end of the airstrip site. A quick descent brought us down farther, to just a few feet above the ground. The dispatcher, another mission friend, knelt on the floor of the airplane. I yelled, "Now!" whereupon he pushed out as many bags as possible through the door before the signal to stop. The drop zone was short that first time. But it lengthened, week by week. Shovels, wheelbarrow components, crowbars, and of course food and mail for Dick . . . out they went!

He always recovered the mailbag first.

Dick's wife, Audrey, and his four wonderful kids, paid a high price for the Bosavi airstrip. But they paid it willingly. For they knew it was more than simply an airstrip. This was a down payment on the hearts of thousands of those Bosavi people.

What a great day of celebration it was when I made the very first landing on the Bosavi airstrip. The joy and amazement on the faces . . . the yelling . . . I shall never forget it.

They jostled with each other to get near my machine. They compared impressions as they stroked its cold, smooth surface. As I gazed out upon that sea of laughing, smiling brown faces, I saw him. I saw a felt hat.

I saw weariness on his face.

Soon, a young Australian family made Bosavi their home and began a program of health, education, language acquisition, and literacy. And they began to teach of the Word of God.

The Los Angeles Hilton is a long way from the rain forest of Bosavi. Most guests there would feel very uncomfortable if left at the Bosavi airstrip. To some, it would be like landing on another planet! But how would a Bosavi villager feel in the glitz and polish of the Hilton?

It was in 1991 that Jo and I drove from our Redlands home to Los Angeles to meet an Australian friend staying at the Hilton. We were delighted to find that he was traveling with a delegation of leaders from Papua New Guinea. There was much laughter and lively conversation as we shared with these men the happy memories of our many years in their beautiful country. They were very sophisticated, fluent in English, perfectly at ease in this renowned international hotel.

But in the background, one of the delegation stood quietly. He was shy and waited until some of the others moved away before stepping forward to speak to us.

Changing from English into the pidgin of his homeland, he asked Jo and me about our life in Papua New Guinea. His dark eyes were searching our faces as he asked about our work. Then, all of a sudden, when I mentioned my role in flying, his face instantly lit up with joy and recognition.

"Now I know who you are," he said. "I recognize your face. From Bosavi. I was there when you dropped that cargo from your airplane. I worked for months on that airstrip! I cleared away bushes and trees! For weeks—for months—we waited for the day when the airplane could land among us. All those weeks as you flew by we longed to meet you, to touch you, to touch your airplane. You brought food for Mr. Donaldson. You brought medicines for us. You brought us the help we needed so desperately. When the airstrip was made, you brought the Briggs family to live among us. That changed our lives."

And so he told us the Donaldson story from his perspective. It was not a story of a foreign religion being foisted upon a reluctant people. It was a story of a transformed people, a people no longer enshrouded in darkness, no longer behind the barriers of awful isolation and the stigma of cannibalism. It was a wonderful story of liberation, of an accelerated transition from the Stone Age to the twentieth century.

More importantly, he explained, it was the story of the Bosavi people of Papua New Guinea coming to realize that God was real, that he was the answer to their deepest need.

Our Bosavi friend told of his early education in a rough bush school at Bosavi. He talked of the influence of those missionaries and how they had brought an end to the fear that had bound the people for so long. He told us of how he had listened to the missionaries' stories—white man's stories—at first. He spoke of how it was that in time those same stories were really relevant and meaningful to him and demanded a personal response. He told us of the day he committed his life to Jesus.

He placed one hand over his heart and his other over mine, and then, clasping his hands together he said, "We come from different places, but we belong to each other."

As we parted, this dignified Papua New Guinean leader shook our hands with a beaming smile. In the opulence of the atrium of the Los Angeles Hilton we celebrated the wonder of the relationship we shared—in Christ.

I doubt if Dick Donaldson has ever been in the Los Angeles Hilton.

But it seemed to me that, somehow, he was represented there that night.

I could almost see his smile . . . under a felt hat! ✸

Chapter Nine
··· Skin-Deep Fear ···

God is love. Whoever lives in love lives in God, and God in him. . . . There is no fear in love. But perfect love drives out fear.

1 JOHN 4:16, 18

These were not ordinary passengers, these four Samberigi men. Brown-skinned and muscular, they were mountain men of Papua New Guinea's southern highlands. But on this day they exhibited none of the strength and confidence that would mark them as warriors who should be taken seriously. They carried no weapons.

They were sick and needed treatment. The small mission clinic at Samberigi was insufficient, and knowing that I was planning to fly across the mountains to the north coast, the station nurse asked me to drop these men off along the way. Mendi, about twenty minutes flying to the northwest, had a regional hospital.

As I fastened their seatbelts, I explained as best I could what they should expect on this short flight. But they appeared very uneasy. This was to be their first flight ever. Even for the uninitiated, flying in Papua New Guinea is often a daunting experience. To these tribesmen, who had grown up in the Stone Age, it may be nothing short of terrifying. I noticed the deteriorating weather and thought it could be a daunting experience for me!

Soon after takeoff, light rain began to paint its peculiar patterns on the windshield. Earlier, on the way up from Wasua, my home base on the Fly River, the weather had been reasonably good. At least at a higher altitude. But now the clouds grew ominous atop the mountain peaks. If I climbed above them, it would be difficult to find a way down again. Particularly in the relatively confined space of the Mendi valley.

I headed northwest, tracing the winding path of the mighty Erave River gorge. To the left and to the right majestic peaks filled the sky. On a clear day this steep gorge would present a vista of great beauty. Today, the light was a diffused gray, the river white and turbulent. Misty rain, whipped by mountain winds, produced a strange, matted effect upon the valley walls, and the higher ridges were enshrouded in cloud. From the cockpit of my Cessna it almost seemed as if I was flying into the throat of a very inhospitable gray tunnel.

I noticed a narrow space between the cloud and the ridge to my right and made a quick turn into the next valley with the wheels of the aircraft almost touching the ridgetop. I flew east along that valley, planning to regain my track farther up. Thus, in a zigzag fashion, valley by valley, I made my way toward Mendi.

For a while I wondered whether I would find Mendi at all. I wished that I had not agreed to make this diversion. It would have been simple to fly to the south out of Samberigi for a few miles to climb above the clouds, then to negotiate a way through the mountains to Wewak, my final destination.

Totally absorbed as the minutes ticked by, I paid no attention to my passengers. Suddenly I heard a sound coming from the backseat. It was a low, drawn-out moan! I turned back.

There in the backseat, locked together in an embrace of abject fear, were my three mountain men. Their three black, curly heads were close together, their faces beaded with perspiration. Three pairs of arms were locked together. And staring back at me, three terror-filled pairs of eyes. They were speechless with fear. And my faltering words of encouragement did little to comfort them.

If this flight's tough for me, how must they be feeling? I thought.

I glanced across to check on my fourth passenger, sitting in the frontseat. He, however, had a completely different demeanor. I was surprised. He was staring ahead, contemplative and detached. Even casual.

"Yu no gat pret?" I asked him. ("Aren't you afraid?")

He turned and looked squarely into my eyes. His response was slow and deliberate. I think he'd asked himself the same question.

"Skin bilong mi tasol I pret." ("Only my skin is afraid.")

What? Only his skin?

I talked on.

"So only your skin is afraid?" I asked. "What about the rest of you?"

Pointing out of the window, he answered in his pidgin English with one of the most expressive and profound statements I have ever heard.

"I see the mountains," he said. "They are so close." He gestured with a wave of his hand.

"I see the trees and the rocks as they rush by. I see the rain, and I hear it beating on the glass. I see the clouds all around us. All I see brings fear to me. I didn't know that this big bird of yours shook like this as it flew along. There is much to be afraid of here."

Then with a smile he continued, "But my fear is only as deep as my skin."

"What about the rest of you?" I asked again. "What about under your skin?"

"I am not afraid under my skin," he said. "You see, I know the One who made the mountains. I know the One who made the rocks and the trees. I know the One who made the clouds and the rain for today. He has told me that I don't need to be afraid. Why? Because he lives in me. Inside my skin. And he has promised never to leave me. Because of that, I am not afraid."

He smiled at me. I grinned back at him, incredulous. What a fantastic "show and tell" of true, heaven-sent faith.

Fear was understandable in this situation. It was absolutely consuming his three friends in the backseat. But not him.

Fear was not granted entry beneath his skin. God was there.

We are told in the Bible that a great mystery, hidden for generations, has been made known to those who know God, who belong to him. That mystery is "Christ in you, the hope of glory." My Samberigi friend also demonstrated another truth.

The "Christ in you" is the victor over fear.

But it has to be believed. That is the faith part. Faith translates truth into reality. My Papua New Guinean passenger proved that to me on that flight to Mendi. His faith in this indwelling God worked! Fear does not have to infiltrate the person in whom the Spirit of Christ lives.

The lesson for me that day was all the more meaningful as it was delivered by this unique man, this extraordinary teacher. He had never sat in a classroom. He had never studied at a seminary. But he knew God—and his faith was firm. The situation in which he found himself was far beyond any previous experience he had had. It was certainly beyond his control. It was as far removed from his cultural norm, his daily environment, and his comfort zone as one could possibly imagine. It was terrifying for his friends. But his belief in God gave him the ability to cope.

"Skin tasol"—only skin needs to be afraid!

We who live in what could be described as the more sophisticated world also encounter circumstances beyond our control. We too find ourselves operating outside our comfort zone. Our fear may not be generated in a small airplane negotiating the weather-filled high mountains of some faraway tropical country. Our testing place may be in the arena of a relationship that is damaged to a point where agony of heart seems perpetual. It may come because of painful tensions in marriage or in the agonizing grief and loss of someone deeply loved. It may be the nagging worry over wayward children. It may be a medical diagnosis of a disease that has the power to threaten and even end life. It may be in the gut-wrenching tension of business. Or on the erosion of financial security. A host of things can bring great fear to our lives, fear that so easily will permeate the very fiber of our being, far deeper than our skin, and leave us wondering whether there is any hope of survival.

The God of heaven had become the personal God of my Samberigi passenger. And, now, his fear was only on the surface—skin deep. Because not only was he able to understand great and profound truth, but he was also applying it to life. Rare? Sadly, all too rare. But available, nonetheless, to all. "Fear not. For I am with you," says the Lord. "For I have not given you a spirit of fear, but of love, and a sound mind."

I still like the way my friend put it.

"Skin bilong mi tasol I pret." ✶

Chapter Ten

··· Of Cows, Cans, ···
and Communion Wine

OF COWS . . . .

Put cows in my airplane? Never!

Mine was a special plane. It had a unique role. It carried very important people. Yes, it carried a lot of general cargo as well. But cows? No way!

I wasn't in the cattle transportation business.

I looked after my airplane meticulously and with loving care. I cleaned it regularly, even polished it from time to time. It wasn't a cattle truck!

Besides, I knew nothing about cows. A boy from the suburbs of Sydney, not the country, I was no cowboy. The closest I came to being a cowboy was at the local movie theatre every Saturday afternoon when my friends and I sat enthralled with the heroic exploits of Roy Rogers and John Wayne.

Every year as kids, we went to the Royal Easter Show in Sydney, and while it was fun to watch the cowboys rope and tie calves at the evening rodeo and wonder at the craziness of men who rode humongous bulls that looked incredibly fierce and dangerous, it was not a world I understood—or even wanted to understand. As I walked through the buildings at the showgrounds where the thoroughbred cattle were on display,

I didn't care for the way they glared at me through the horizontal bars of their prisonlike stalls. It was obvious they didn't like me. I certainly didn't like them—the way they smelled and especially what they dropped on the floor.

In very truth, I was no cowboy.

Put cows in my plane? Not if it was up to me.

But the request had come from a friend on his remote station 150 miles away. "I've arranged to buy a couple of heifers from the Lutheran Agricultural Station near you. They'll be a great help in our agriculture school. Could you please bring them in? Bring them in one at a time. I'll cover the cost."

But it took many weeks to get approval to take the heifers across regional borders, and in those weeks, these two young members of the bovine family ate and ate—and got fatter and fatter! They surely didn't look like heifers to me when I first saw them being driven along the road toward the airstrip. They were full-grown cows to my inexperienced eye. The pride of the Lutheran herd!

With a sense of impending doom I asked the agriculturist who had brought them, "How am I going to get them into the plane? Who's going to help?"

His reply did nothing for my sagging enthusiasm. "I'll help you," he said. "We'll find others to give you a hand." It sounded to me as if I was to be in charge!

I was to learn many lessons about cows that day.

For a start, cows don't lie down just because you want them to. In fact, they strongly resist any effort to make them do so. They resisted absolutely everything I wanted to do! I was exhausted by the time we had the first one lying on the ground so that it could be tied up with the endless lengths of strong rope I had bought for the occasion.

And by then I smelled just like my reluctant passenger.

The ten or so near-naked mountain warriors, who had been recruited to help as they were walking down the road, lay straddling the cow, thinking this was great fun. To them, this was just another kind of pig—a very big one, a very strong one. Strangely enough, cleanliness and order having long since departed, I was beginning to think it was rather fun as well. The cow was the only one thinking otherwise.

It took a long while to get her into the plane. Bellows of protest during that hour had attracted a veritable crowd of people who now stood around laughing and offering enthusiastic advice. Great entertainment for them. As I sweated and strained, I thought back to those men who roped and tied the calves at the Royal Easter Show. I was glad they weren't watching!

Neither of my passengers would stand on the scales for me, but I guessed they weighed about 350–400 pounds each. It was a pretty rough guess. Getting the first cow into the plane had been such a complicated business, and I was such a disgusting mess that the thought of repeating this performance the following day had little appeal. It would be better for me, I decided, though maybe not for the cows, if I threw in the other one as well.

The thought that I might kill two birds, as it were, with the one stone had interesting connotations. Little did I know.

After a couple of hours, all was ready. My unwilling passengers were on board, trussed up with so much rope that it looked as if they had run into a giant spider web. As well as the rope that tied horn to heel and shoulder to shank, I had covered the entire wretched, struggling load with the heavy nylon mesh net that I always used to secure cargo in the plane. Two pairs of eyes, however, revealed something less than a contented state. They glared at me with malevolent stares from within their netting prison. Out of two slobbering mouths came a terrible noise, and what was worse, these two large, brown, hairy creatures had demonstrated their absolute derision and antagonism toward me by depositing a disgusting and horribly smelly mess on the clean floor of my polished Cessna even before I commenced the takeoff.

This flight needed no delays, no diversions.

Climbing toward the high pass of the nearby mountains, however, it soon became obvious that my passengers were somehow in cahoots with the weather to take revenge on me. The far peaks were covered in billowing, darkening cloud. It would not be easy to find a way through. I tried hard, very hard, and even harder as I contemplated the prospect of having to land at an intermediate strip somewhere along the route and allowing my passengers to disembark. The thought of overnighting somewhere with them to await better weather the next day … was just too much.

There seemed no way through. In absolute frustration I radioed my wife to inquire about the weather back home. At least there were agriculturists there who could be baby-sitters. "Don't come back here," Jo advised. "Since you took off the weather has really deteriorated. I don't think you could get back anyway."

Wonderful!

Why did I say I would do this job?

Realizing my predicament—for these were very, very smart cows— they began to play their part to make the situation worse. They kicked and jerked, and kicked again, over and over until the plane began to shake, and I became increasingly concerned. If they forced their way out of their leg restraints, their strong legs could surely make a hole through the aircraft or at least do considerable damage.

And worse, if they did struggle free of the ropes and net and try to stand up, there just wouldn't be enough room in the plane for the three of us. We could crash!

And I didn't want to slink sheepishly (!) into heaven, smelling like this!

What a mess . . . in more ways than one. I really didn't know quite what to do.

Then . . . the penny dropped! I had the solution.

I remembered back to my days as a jet-fighter pilot. On every flight I depended on oxygen, as most flights were done above thirty-five thousand feet. I recalled the first day, in 1956, when my cadet class, feeling like guinea pigs, went through various tests in the decompression chamber at the Royal Australian Air Force's School of Aviation Medicine. In an effort to teach us about the dangers of oxygen deprivation, anoxia, half the class would not be provided oxygen as the chamber was "taken up" to an equivalent of thirty-five thousand feet. The rest of the class breathed oxygen all the way, only taking off their oxygen masks when finally reaching the same altitude. It was a fascinating and salutary lesson to see and feel the different, but sure and deadly effects of anoxia upon the human body.

But these were cows, for heaven's sake!

Nevertheless, they needed to be quieted down. And I needed a few thousand feet of extra altitude to get over the weather.

Making no mention, of course, of the needs of my bovine passengers, I called the Civil Aviation authorities with my intention to climb to at least sixteen thousand feet for a while to get over the weather. Taking the yellow mask from under my seat and turning on the oxygen flow, I began the long climb toward the blue sky I could see above the towering weather.

Amazingly, the cows became quite restful. They settled down to nap for a while!

Keeping a close watch to make sure that their heaving chests remained heaving, I scraped over the lowest section of cloud and, now able to see the low country ahead, began a long, slow descent toward my destination. I wanted it to be slow!

It was with a confident air that I delivered my two passengers to their new owner about forty minutes later. With a little help from some of his friends, we were easily able to unload them. They were drowsy and docile, so glad their journey was over.

As they were led off along the jungle track toward the meadow that was to be their new home, they turned around to look at me, one last time. Their brown eyes were soft and tranquil—a little sleepy, it seemed.

I think they quite liked me!

I think God was smiling.

Of Cans . . . .

I did some stupid things in airplanes when I was young. I remember looking death in the face more than once flying a jet fighter, and if I had died on any of those occasions, it would have been totally my own fault. I was only twenty years old . . . but that's another story.

In my MAF years I remember only one occasion when death seemed at hand. It wasn't during takeoff or landing—which made it even more unexpected. It was while cruising in a clear blue sky on a very routine flight. . . .

The MAF warehouse at Wewak was always full of freight and supplies. As quickly as we flew them out to the four corners of the country, the merchants and shipping agents in the seaport town where we lived would bring more in.

Every morning our client missions would make requests on the radio regarding things that were most needed from the cargo bay where their supplies were stored. The mailbag was always the top priority. Usually after mail came the frozen food stored in the large freezer in the hangar. After these specially requested items were weighed and manifested, it was simply a matter of trying to lower the pile of stuff that remained.

My load for the flight on this particular day was fairly typical. I had been into Wewak for maintenance on my airplane and was headed home. En route I planned to drop most of my cargo at a mission station near Wapenamanda where we lived. There was mail. There were fresh vegetables, cartons and drums of canned food, educational and medical supplies. Everything was individually weighed and marked, then listed on the manifest. Very routine.

The national workers at Wewak were very good at loading the airplane. They had worked for MAF for many years and knew exactly how to ensure that the aircraft's center of gravity was within prescribed limits. The airplane was fueled for the planned time of the flight plus the required sixty minutes of reserve. A phone call to the Civil Aviation authorities assured that the flight plan was in order. The airplane was in good shape. The cargo load was within limits and correctly stowed and restrained. I climbed up on the wing-strut to personally check that the fuel contents were as I had requested and that the tank caps were securely closed. Ready to go.

As I climbed aboard I felt confident that nothing had been neglected; however, I did notice that the load was bulky. It filled the entire cabin ... but that was not unusual. I tried to move some of the cargo stowed right at shoulder level behind the pilot's seat, but it was too firmly restrained, so I squeezed my way around it, sat down, and began to run through the pre-start checklist and get the flight under way.

Takeoff and climb-out were uneventful. The weather was great. I could see the mountains a hundred miles away. I had an hour and a half to go, and the prospect was for a very normal flight. Probably a little boring.

From ten thousand feet the Sepik River looked like a huge wandering serpent as it curled its way through the region. Motorized canoes left their V-wakes on its brown surface. The ground was freckled with the shadows of the light fair-weather tufts of cloud at about five thousand feet. I checked my position and my time to the river. On time. On track. Jo had told me on the radio that the weather at Wapenamanda was also clear, so it seemed like a flight that would be uneventful and soon forgotten.

Very routine. Yes, rather boring.

Then, in a split second ... there was an incredible explosion. The noise was literally deafening.

Everything went white. There was no instrument panel, no cargo, no airplane, no view of the river or the mountains, no cloud. Inside, outside, above, and below—everything was white. Disorientation began to set in. I felt as if I could not breathe. I didn't know where I was.

My first thought was that I had been involved in a midair collision, that there had been an almighty impact there at ten thousand feet over the Sepik River. But I could see no red fire as my aircraft burned, no pall of black smoke. There was no heat, no light, no pain. Everything remained— just white. And totally quiet. I was enveloped, entombed in a dense, white silent cloud, and I felt strangely, unusually, comfortable.

This must be heaven. So this is what it is really like, I immediately thought. But I sensed that I was fully conscious, and I wondered, *What on earth is happening to me?*

I have no idea how much time passed before, from the impenetrable nothingness in front of me, a dim, surreal impression of a ghostly white instrument panel began to appear, coming slowly into focus. And as the strange whiteness began to move about in front of my eyes, I could see that the airspeed was still at its correct 120 knots, the altimeter still read ten thousand feet, and the turn-and-balance instrument was indicating that the airplane was flying straight and level.

I peered ahead, confused, dazed. Then gradually I became aware of something else. It was the faint noise of the aircaft's engine. Slowly it got louder, and louder—until I could hear it quite clearly. And it sounded absolutely normal. In fact, everything was normal—at least as far as the airplane was concerned.

But a strange feeling of dryness gagged in my throat and nostrils.

What happened? What had happened to me?

By now, I could see my two hands appearing out of the whiteness. They were still on the control wheel holding the airplane straight and level.

I looked down at my arms, my legs, and my thighs.

Aha . . . I had the answer.

On each of my legs and arms was a ridge of . . . pure white flour! Like tiny avalanches in tiny snowy mountains, flour was falling to the floor as I moved. The peaks of the flour crests were about three inches high, right along my legs and arms. I shook my right hand, and the air in front of me, which had begun to clear, was once again filled with a cloud of flour blowing around like a minute snowstorm.

I smiled, then laughed loudly, almost hysterical with relief, as I realized what had happened.

I wasn't in heaven. I hadn't gone suddenly, in a catastrophic crash, to meet my Maker.

Turning around, I saw the evidence. A strong, steel can holding twenty-two pounds of flour that had been wedged just behind my right shoulder had burst apart in an explosive failure. It was ripped apart from top to bottom along the seam. Pressure differential had found a fault in the can's manufacture, causing a huge, instantaneous explosive decompression. And in that split second, twenty-two pounds of fine white powder had been atomized, discharged with tremendous pressure into the restricted space of that fully loaded aircraft cabin. The noise had temporarily deafened me. The flour was everywhere, filling my mouth, my ears, and my nostrils.

I slid down in the seat to catch my reflection in the glass of the instrument panel, and sure enough, I had a cone of white flour, reaching almost to the roof, on my head. Small rivulets of flour ran down through my eyebrows at the front and under the collar of my shirt at the back, giving me extra padding against the seat. No wonder I had felt so comfortable.

Thinking that I should fly straight home instead of to my planned destination, I stayed as "still as a mouse" so as not to disturb my hilarious appearance. I flew the airplane ever so gently down into our home valley and did as smooth a landing as I could. I wanted Jo to see what it would be like to be married to the abominable snowman or, at least, to see me in this hysterically funny state, hair and eyebrows whitened in some kind of premature aging, dressed in ghostly white clothing, and wearing a cone-shaped hat of flour on my head.

Did I hear a heavenly chuckle?

Of Communion Wine . . . :

It was hot in the noonday sun at Madang—very hot. One didn't need an atlas to confirm that we weren't far from the equator. The air was so humid. This was doldrums time—there was not even a suspicion of breeze.

Loading the airplane in the heat that day, I looked as if someone had squirted me with a hose or I had fallen in the ocean. And either would have been welcome.

The demanding task of loading a huge, very heavy wooden cask of wine into the Cessna wasn't helping either. I could see people laughing at me, passengers walking across the tarmac to board a couple of old DC3s, the workhorse of Papua New Guinea's development in those days. "Look at that crazy guy," they must have thought, "dripping with sweat, rolling a gigantic keg across an airport tarmac!"

Why couldn't the Lutherans use grape juice in nice small cans for Communion wine like most other people? I thought to myself. *Why does it have to be the genuine article, shipped all the way from Germany? And if they wanted this stuff, couldn't they buy it in bottles rather than in this ridiculous, enormous barrel? Why had I drawn the short straw to have had to come down here in this sticky, stinking heat to pick it up?*

The thought of that straw—be it short or long—came to mind again later in the day.

They were great friends, these Lutherans. We so much enjoyed living on their base at Wapenamanda. Flying for them was always fun . . . and very rewarding. But they were different. I thought about my upbringing. Not a drop of alcohol had ever crossed the lips of my dad or my mom. We had been brought up to believe that one taste of the forbidden strong drink would certainly land us on the threshold of Hades! Our Lutheran friends thought somewhat differently. No grape juice for them at Communion. Only genuine, best-quality port wine would suffice. The real stuff. From a faraway German vineyard.

So here I was, struggling to get this ancient wooden monster containing fifty gallons of the stuff across the tarmac. I had no idea how I was going to get the keg into the airplane, to lift it the three feet up over the sill of the door. I knew it would have to be carried lying down. It would not fit standing up.

It took quite a while, a number of people, and two large lengths of timber before the barrel was finally rolled aboard. The rest of my cargo was loaded around and on top of it.

The cool air through the vent system was a welcome relief as I climbed out of Madang toward the mountains. The worst of the exercise was over. There would be plenty of help to unload this item of sinfulness. But as I looked ahead I realized that perhaps the worst wasn't over. In the couple of hours I had spent on the ground at Madang the weather had deteriorated markedly. The horizon had changed from the serrated blue-black beauty of the mountain range into the crisp white outline of developing cumulonimbus clouds. *I certainly won't be able to get through there at ten thousand feet,* I thought.

It wasn't too bad, however. I found myself skimming the tops of cloud at about thirteen thousand feet, and a call to Jo at home told me that the weather was quite fine at Wapenamanda. With the background of the smooth-running Continental engine and listening to the chatter on the radio, I felt quite relaxed. My shirt was dry again. At last I was cool. This was my final flight for the day. All was well.

Suddenly, there was a loud, sharp sound, almost like a rifle shot.

Whatever was that? I looked around at the full load of cargo behind me. Nothing appeared to have moved.

But then I heard—and smelled—the answer. Both at the same time.

The noise was—"Glug . . . glug . . . glug . . . glug."

The smell was—sweet, enticing, intoxicating!

That huge wooden cask with its fifty gallons of prized port wine, all the way from Germany, was slowly emptying itself into my aircraft. The bung had failed, flying like a bullet to the back of the plane.

And I could do nothing about it.

I couldn't pull over to the side of the road and block the hole. I couldn't call upon the services of a loadmaster or another crewmember to stand it up and stop it from emptying itself all through my Cessna.

I could do nothing—so I simply kept going.

It suddenly crossed my mind that if this stuff, this dreaded product of a faraway vineyard, really tasted as good as it smelled, my family had missed out on all kinds of great things all those years. Maybe we hadn't been so smart!

The picture of what my airplane might look like to those on the ground was quite intriguing. No Cessna like mine flies high enough to make a condensation trail high in the sky as does a high-flying jet airliner from time to time. But this was no condensation trail of freezing water vapor. After all, any airline pilot could make one of those. This was different. I was making history here, laying down a condensation trail—and a red one at that . . . of prized German wine.

It was quite sad to think that no one appreciated this wondrous phenomenon.

I don't know whether one can get drunk on the smell of wine, but I thought about that, too.

As I considered the situation, it occurred to me that my ignorance of the nature of wine casks had contributed, at least in part, to my present predicament. I knew nothing about anything to do with wine. Had I known more I would have recognized the necessity to load the keg with the bung at the top. Then, I suppose, I may have had only a few gallons of wine in the plane . . . a few more when I lowered the nose to descend. But in my ignorance I had rolled the barrel in with its bung at the bottom, and I had the whole nine yards—no, the whole fifty gallons—of that entrancingly smelling stuff sloshing around in the bowels of my plane.

As I eventually lowered the nose to descend, I could hear it swishing around, finding its way to the front, wetting the heels of my shoes. By this time I was beginning to think about the awesome amount of work this wretched, now-empty keg had created for me. It was going to be a major task to clean the aircraft. I might have been an ignoramus in the ways of wine, but I knew that it would be terribly corrosive if not totally washed out or otherwise removed.

At the thought of what MAF's chief engineer was going to say to me, or maybe do to me, I grimaced. Not only was he almost paranoid about us keeping our airplanes in pristine condition, he was even more an ultraconservative teetotaler than I. *Would he see the funny side of this?* I wondered. He wouldn't.

He didn't!

After landing at Wapenamanda, I carefully inspected my aromatic aircraft. There was a beautiful, glistening, purple-looking sheen all along the underside of the rear fuselage. Yes, indeed, I must have laid a glorious trail across the blue mountain sky.

I smiled as I wondered whether minute droplets of this wonderfully-smelling brew would have reached the ground, penetrating the heavy forest below. Maybe some primitive hunter caught that aroma and set off at the run to find its source.

Needing a respite from the smell—from the whole, hilarious episode—I drove home to have lunch before I commenced the long task of cleaning up. It would mean taking all the panels out of the floor and washing every single piece of metal, every cable, every pulley. I needed to have a break first. Besides, I wanted to tell Jo all about it.

As I arrived home, my next door neighbor, the pathologist at the mission hospital, was in his front yard. I couldn't help but tell him about the episode before I went inside.

"You mean to tell me that there were fifty gallons of that wonderful stuff washing about in the bowels of your airplane?"

"Not only that, John," I replied. "There are gallons of it still there in the cargo pod under the plane."

My friend, John, a colorful character from the southern U.S., turned around toward his house, cupped his hands to his mouth, and yelled, "Honey . . . get the drinkin' straws. We're goin' to the airport!"

I'm glad God has such a great sense of humor. ✸

PART THREE

Chapter Eleven

··· War ···

He makes wars cease to the ends of the earth; he breaks the bow and shatters the spear, he burns the shields with fire. "Be still, and know that I am God; I will be exalted among the nations, I will be exalted in the earth."

PSALM 46:9–10

In the early sixties, Jo and I, with our two small boys, lived in a very small aluminum house right on the edge of the beach at Wewak, New Guinea. We would walk along the sand. And often, after a storm, we'd see them. Rolling around in the surf, or left at the high-tide mark. Human bones. Perhaps a femur, or a tibia, a scapula, or a curved bone of the rib cage. The fury of a tropical storm would wrest them out of their secret watery graves and deposit them on the sands of Wewak's beaches.

There, above the tide-line, we would dig a hole and bury them.

Whose bones were they?

Did they belong to someone we knew?

The father, perhaps, of a childhood friend?

American? Australian? Perhaps Japanese? We couldn't tell. But this we did know. Some young man, long ago, had set out from a distant home to fight for a cause—and never returned.

A relative of Jo's had been shot down over the sea there in Wewak, toward the last days of the war. His commanding officer had written to the family, describing his bravery as a fighter pilot. "I saw his plane take a hit over Wewak, and I watched it crash into the bay," he wrote.

87

He had been twenty-one years old. Perhaps we had buried one of his bones.

On Saturday afternoons, we would take the kids to a beach called Moem, a few miles to the east. With face mask and snorkel, we would swim for hours in the warm waters of our own tropical aquarium, just a few feet from the shore. The vivid colors of the schools of fish enhanced the spectacular beauty of the coral reefs that paralleled the beach. It was an exotic place, peaceful and secluded.

One particular Saturday, in the late sixties, as we were relaxing there, Michael, Timothy, Jonathan, and Robin hassled us to allow them to go and "explore." The jungle nearby was thick, almost impenetrable, and grew to the water's edge.

Our children were very much at home in the jungle, so we agreed, but with the strong proviso that they go no further than shouting distance. But within a few minutes they bound out of the bush, wildly excited.

To our amazement and horror, they were carrying belts of still-live World War II ammunition. They also had a number of personal identification "dog tags."

"The bullets and these things were all mixed up with the bones," said Michael, our oldest, panting. They led me impatiently to the site of the find.

There, just yards from our picnic site, was the wreckage of what had been a B-24 Liberator bomber. It had lain where it had crashed, hidden for a quarter of a century in the ever-enveloping jungle undergrowth.

With the kids, I sifted through the pieces. Among the broken metal and shards of sun-baked perspex, lay the scattered, whitened bones of the crew.

Who were these men? We talked together about them.

They were men who had loved and had been loved. They were MIAs—missing in action—their loss made all the more poignant because their bodies had never been found. Somebody's sons. Somebody's husbands. Somebody's brothers. Their families had never known how they died or where. Maybe their children still lived in the United States but had no memory of their fathers. Just stories.

When the ID tags and remains were eventually returned to their homeland, undoubtedly, to some degree for the families of the men, there was closure. Perhaps there were official burials in veteran's cemeteries in the United States. Healing tears were shed, I'm sure, as honor was given to those men, lost for so many years.

It was simply a routine operation. To dig a ditch.

But once again, they were there. In the ditch. The national workers found them. Human bones. This time, though, in a line of unmarked graves. It was immediately apparent that these bodies had been haphazardly, even violently, thrown into the ground. There was no dignity. They were not lying in any orderly, respectful way. Each rough grave contained just a mixed-up mess of bones, piled on top of one another. But no skulls. Not one. Each skeleton was without a head. And so they remained, totally unidentifiable, lost victims of a gruesome wartime execution!

Our family was living in Wewak in 1970 when the celebration of the twenty-fifth anniversary of the Japanese surrender to the Allied forces took place. A few miles away, Wom Point had been one of the sites where formal signings of surrender took place. There, at Wom, a white obelisk marked the place where the commanding general of the Japanese forces of the region handed over his sword to the Allied commander.

Hundreds of veterans came from all over the world to commemorate the anniversary. Americans, Australians, and Japanese. And one single man from India. He was the sole survivor of an entire Indian battalion that had been captured on the Malay Peninsula and brought by the Japanese all the way to New Guinea to serve them. At liberation, there were eighteen Indian soldiers left. All of them, save this one man, who was ill at the time, were being transported by air to Rabaul to join a ship back to India when their plane crashed. All were killed.

And so, here, twenty-five years later, former enemies reminisced quietly together. And reconciled. Twenty-five years had brought a lot of healing.

I talked to one middle-aged Japanese lady standing at the periphery of the crowd. She pointed to an area of heaped, crushed coral. "My husband . . . buried here . . . ," she said in her broken English. Then she looked up and, she pointing to fourteen-month-old Chris, sitting on my shoulders, said, "My son . . . little . . . like him . . . when daddy go away. He not remember." But she remembered.

The rivers of Gaudalcanal "ran red with blood" in World War II. I have waded through those rivers and flown over them many times. The Solomon Island people living there had no war of their own. It was a war between other nations, but fought on their land. Their country and villages were devastated. Thousands were killed, and their peaceful way of life was forever changed.

At another place and time of remembrance I visited Gettysburg. Walking in the stillness and silence along the lines of canon that remain in the fields there, I read the plaques. Each one outlined the history of a battle. I felt an almost overwhelming sense of sadness at the thought of the hundreds of thousands of men and women who died in those dark and dreadful days of civil war—all of them Americans.

It seemed that I could almost hear the stirring words of Abraham Lincoln:

> Fourscore and seven years ago our fathers brought forth on this continent, a new nation, conceived in Liberty, and dedicated to the proposition that all men are created equal. Now we are engaged in a great civil war, testing whether that nation, or any

nation so conceived and so dedicated, can long endure.... But in a larger sense, we cannot dedicate—we cannot consecrate—we cannot hallow—this ground. The brave men, living and dead, who struggled here, have consecrated it, far above our poor power to add or detract....

Gettysburg, today, is not only a moving and sensitively presented national cemetery; it is a constant reminder to the American people that civil war must never be allowed to happen again. Never!

It was January 1995. We were driven up the steep, rocky road from Peshawar, Pakistan, through the Khyber Pass into Afghanistan. Rudyard Kipling seemed to speak from every rock, every hill. From a cramped position in an overcrowded minibus there was a panorama across the brown, dry mountains to the faraway peaks of the famed Hindu Kush. But as I looked down into the ravines and canyons, I saw the rusted remains of hundreds of trucks, tanks, and other pieces of military equipment. Afghanistan had been a war zone for generations.

In the streets of Kabul, rows of deserted, ruined buildings bore their own terrible scars of war—holes blasted in thick reinforced concrete, twisted steel girders, empty window frames. I met and shared food with wonderful Afghani people. The children and most of the adults have only known a life of conflict, danger, and pain. The very fabric of the life of Afghanistan is permeated with effects of war. So many have been "child soldiers."

Far too many children today bear arms instead of toys. One, just one, is too many. It must be one of the greatest human rights offenses of modern times. I have seen children, barely in their teens, being driven along dusty roads, uniformed soldiers, with oversized metal helmets too heavy to bear, pressed into active service, desperately trying to look older than their years. They are trained to kill and destroy. They know how to use the sophisticated weaponry they carry. Their childhood has been stolen from them, never to be returned. Years, which should contain fun, learning, and joy, have been taken away. What a perversion of the care-free innocence of all that God meant childhood to be.

Scripture, too, talks of war. Another kind of warfare.

And the people of God today, as they have been throughout time, are involved in this warfare. It is not warfare of nation against nation, of guns and missiles and bombs. It is not fought in the physical realm. But it is warfare, nonetheless. It is spiritual warfare, where the powers of God are arrayed against the powers of evil. Where hope is arrayed against despair.

Looking back on the seasons of my life, I see interesting contrasts and comparisons. My Air Force logbook records three thousand flights. My MAF logbook records more than thirty thousand. In my days of military aviation I helped refine the tools of war, working with the brightest of human minds involved in weapons research. In my days of mission aviation I became involved in that other kind of warfare, the battle for the souls of men.

MAF pilots don't fire guns or rockets. They don't drop bombs. They don't wreak havoc and devastation. But there is a cost. And sometimes the cost is life itself.

There is one remarkable difference.

This war is not just winnable. Its victory is absolute and certain. ✷

Thanks be to God! He gives us the
victory through our Lord Jesus Christ.

1 CORINTHIANS 15:57

Chapter Twelve

···Light Over Darkness···

"I am the light of the world. Whoever follows me will never walk in darkness, but will have the light of life."

JOHN 8:12

* * *

"You are the light of the world . . . let your light shine before men, that they may see your good deeds and praise your Father in heaven."

MATTHEW 5:14,16

In April 1994, Jo and I made a flight from Los Angeles to Johannesburg, South Africa, right at the time the conflict in Rwanda was about to explode. Newspapers and TV reports were full of stories of a terrible human disaster taking place in that beautiful country. Killing sprees were predicted to escalate even further, and there was talk of total genocide. It seemed that the larger nations were doing little to stop this tragedy. A friend told me the previous week that he had seen a mass of corpses bouncing in the foaming water at the base of a waterfall on the Rwanda-Tanzania border.

The agony at Rwanda during that time is now history. It seems beyond belief that eight-hundred-thousand people could have died there in just a hundred days of mad rampage.

At London's Heathrow airport, Jo and I tried to keep abreast of the news in Rwanda. We had arrived there, already weary, at 6:00 A.M. Now, we were facing a fourteen-hour layover before the flight to Africa. What news we could get was very disturbing.

An evacuation on a massive scale was taking place. A large proportion of the Rwandan population, mainly Hutu people, was seeking safety in neighboring Zaire. More than a million had already crossed the border at Goma and Bukavu. More were expected. The increasing danger was that there would be an outbreak of disease among the refugees in the appalling and totally unsanitary conditions. It was a dark time in African history, a political and tribal conflict that few people outside of Rwanda could ever hope to understand.

The TV monitors in the airport showed video confirming our worst fears. Not only was Goma and the surrounding countryside occupied by up to one and a half million Rwandan refugees, but cholera had broken out there. Disenfranchised, hungry, traumatized people, many of whom had witnessed unbelievable horror in recent days, were dying by the thousands.

While still at Heathrow I confirmed my plans to fly on to Goma from Johannesburg. We had a conference to attend, but it was more important that I visit MAF staff in eastern Zaire. A time of intense pressure, I needed to ascertain what part MAF could play in the huge relief effort that would be necessary. I also just wanted to "be there" with our Zaire staff. Superb people.

We had been "on the road" twenty-eight hours already and had at least another twelve to go before we touched down at Jan Smuts airport in South Africa. Finally we boarded, and after a further two-hour technical delay, the aircraft was pushed back from the gate. Great, now we might get a few hours sleep.

The captain, having first apologized for the delay, said, "I'm afraid that we are expecting some rather bumpy weather during the first few hours of our long flight tonight. Other flights have experienced severe turbulence. After we cross into North Africa, though, it should settle down and be calm for the rest of the flight." Just what we needed!

For those first two hours the aircraft seemed to chase the thunderstorms! Lightning cracked all around us. The cabin crew remained tightly strapped into their seats along with the white-knuckled passengers. As we bounced around like a cork in the surf, I noticed a phenomenon that I had seldom seen since my Air Force days. Tiny flames of static electricity known to airmen as "Saint Elmo's fire" dashed across the outside of the windows and along the skin of the aircraft.

There were sighs of relief when the weather finally calmed down and all on board tried to rest for the remaining nine or ten hours of the flight.

Very few of the exhausted passengers bothered to watch the in-flight movie. Most tried to grab a few hours of sleep. Wide awake, I eased out of my seat and made my way down to the back of the plane. After standing there for a while, I lowered the small collapsible cabin-crew seat fixed to the rear bulkhead and strapped myself in. I had the small, square rear-door window all to myself. But there was nothing to be seen in the darkness of the night outside apart from the regular flash of the airplane's wingtip navigation light.

Hours must have gone by when, suddenly, something caught my attention in the sky, breaking the intense darkness outside. Faraway, hundreds of miles to the east, small flashes of lightning like tiny, white fireworks burst in the night. I knew, however, that at the actual location of the storm, which probably sat over the center or the east of Zaire, they would not be tiny flashes. These were crashing, brilliant, thundering bursts of power, probably generated by as violent a weather system as the one that had made this huge aircraft seem so vulnerable just a few hours ago over the Mediterranean. But from my small square window I could only see the black darkness with intermittent flashes, minute specks of white light out there, somewhere. It was fascinating.

This storm could well have been pouring its fury upon the million and a half refugee Rwandans huddled together on the bare, black lava-rock around Goma. There would be no shelter for them.

And from my unique vantage point at forty thousand feet, I prayed for them.

I watched the eastern sky begin to lighten.

The night had been long, but the sun was coming.

In the awakening dawn, the intermittent spots of white lightning flashes disappeared. I'm sure the storm didn't cease. It was just that the light that was coming was more intense, brighter than that faraway lightning. The greater new light simply chased the smaller light away!

It was a spectacular dawn. A wonderful kaleidoscope of color seemed to reach up over the darkness that covered the mass of the African continent, and then descend upon it. As it had chased away the random flashes of the faraway lightning, so it now chased away the darkness across that entire landmass. Night gave way to day, a clear, bright, shining day, revealing the wonderful vista of beautiful Africa. Great rivers, majestic mountains, vast plains, and lush jungles.

Everything that I could now see had been there all the time, but it had been enshrouded in darkness.

Jesus' words "I am the light of the world" filled my mind.

Just as the sun that morning chased away the darkness of a long night, revealing a panorama of great beauty, I knew that even the horrendous and agonizing darkness of Rwanda could be driven away by the light of God's love. I prayed again for the people of Rwanda. I prayed that the greater light—that "eternal light"—would shine into their darkness.

As I sat there, alone alongside "my" window that morning, I felt a special closeness to the One who is the "light of the world." I offered to him my deep thanks that his plans had included me. I thanked him for deeming me worthy of a place in the light.

But this unique "devotion at dawn" was not over. Some other scriptures came to mind. Interesting words that the apostle John recorded Jesus as having said. "While I am in the world I am the light of the world."

While I am in the world? I thought. *What did that mean?*

Then in Matthew's record, another of the sayings of Jesus.

"*You* are the light of the world."

Twelve men, and ordinary men at that—the light of the world?

I pondered the two similar yet very different statements. It seemed almost blasphemous to take upon ourselves something that was true of the Lord Jesus. But it was Jesus who said it. I reconciled for myself this seeming contradiction. Because those who are committed to him become channels through which the eternal and divine light of the world shines, he infuses his life into those who follow him. In truth, they do become the light of the world.

Divine delegation, divine empowerment. But what responsibility!

Two days later I stood on the black lava-rock of Goma, Zaire. Hundreds of thousands of Rwandan refugees stood or sat, shoulder to shoulder, as far as I could see. There was no shelter for them other than small, blue plastic tarpaulins, distributed by United Nations workers. There was overwhelming suffering, total bewilderment, and agony of soul.

One particular little boy stood out. Before crossing the border from Rwanda, he had seen both of his parents hacked to pieces with a machete in front of his eyes. When he arrived, the relief workers told me, he was talking. But he ceased talking the next day, and they couldn't get him to say another word. For four days now, he had been standing in the open air at the relief center, staring vacantly into space. He was living a horrible nightmare.

By the time I arrived, the relief effort was already in full swing. Military aircraft from all the major nations were landing one after the other to disgorge hundreds of tons of food and clothing. High in the sky tanker airplanes were refueling the U.S. and other military airplanes as they headed back to Europe and America to reload. Men in camouflage fatigues were everywhere. Helicopters whipped dust into clouds as they took off to distribute food.

I watched American and French military bulldozers cover a huge hole, the mass grave where thousands of unidentified Rwandan cholera victims had been buried. The drivers wore masks over their faces. It didn't smell nice there.

Amidst this overwhelming horror and tragedy, my thoughts returned to "my" sunrise.

And to the light of the world.

A beautiful young lady, standing out in a predominantly male crowd at the airport, told me that she had come from Manchester, England, to help out. "I'm a trauma nurse," she said, "and I simply couldn't stand to see the footage of this tragedy on the television without responding. I resigned my job yesterday and flew down here on the evening plane. I've come to do what I can for as long as it takes. This awful tragedy of human life must break God's heart."

The light of the world. It was there—in her! She had come, bringing the light with her.

A team of African doctors and nurses who had flown thousands of miles from their mission hospital in West Africa were achieving small miracles, saving lives in a hastily erected tent clinic. They too had brought the light of the world. It shone through them as it did through so many others driven there by a godly compassion.

When we had landed at Goma the previous day, we had taxied our small MAF Cessna between huge military transport planes from many countries that were disgorging tons of food and relief supplies. An American missionary who had been in that area for fifty years met us. Tears streamed down his face. "I'm so glad you've come," he said. My reply was probably rather flippant. I thought the meager few hundred pounds of supplies in our airplane were less than insignificant. "Yes, but the difference is that you are here to care for the spirits of the people."

You see, MAF also carries the light of the world.

Jesus, the light of the world, stands central in history as in eternity, to drive away darkness.

And it is he who said, "You are the light of the world." ✮

Chapter Thirteen

···Timbuktu···

> "I, even I, am the LORD,
> and apart from me there
> is no Savior."
>
> ISAIAH 43:11

Timbuktu. What a name!

When I was a boy, Timbuktu was an imaginary place, a fantasy, created by writers of adventure stories for boys. A favorite "rainy day" book of my childhood described the sandy streets, the ancient mud-brick dwellings, and the shimmering heat of its desert horizons.

So when, in 1987, I found myself wandering those same sandy streets with Jo, I smiled, recalling much-loved tales and legends of faraway places. For this was no work of fiction, no fanciful excursion of the imagination. This was real. We were actually there, in Timbuktu. Fascinating and exotic still, Timbuktu in reality conjured up images of an adventure. Even for grown-up boys.

Timbuktu is an ancient place, steeped in the mystical charm of an ancient desert culture. To its twenty-five thousand inhabitants, it is home. Muslim pilgrims from all over Africa visit the magnificent centuries-old mosque that stands there with heavy wooden beams protruding through the mud-brick outside walls. A revered place, a holy shrine in the world of Islam.

For century upon century, camel travelers and passersby have stopped there to rest and gather supplies. To them, Timbuktu stands as a welcome respite from the slow, laborious plod across the wastelands of the Sahara.

It is also a place of rich heritage and history. In the twelfth century, one of the world's most prestigious universities was established there. The nearby Niger River also made this a verdant place, a place of luxuriant growth, of trade and wealth. Then, the sands of Sahara were still a distance to the north.

Over the centuries, however, the sand has moved inexorably closer with each passing year. From the north the Sahara has made its advance, inching its way south, slowly robbing Timbuktu of the richness, the greenery, the fertility. Today it stands remote, magnificent. A city engulfed in sand. Yet it remains still a place of great pride for the people of the Republic of Mali.

Nouh Ag Infa Yatara, "Pastor Nouh," one of the finest young men I have ever met, was our guide that day. A dark-skinned man of great dignity and presence. Nouh is a shepherd. A shepherd of believers. In a city of 25,000, Nouh is the pastor of just twenty people who name the name of Jesus.

Nouh's story of coming to faith in Christ is almost beyond belief.

As a small boy he was caught stealing vegetables. The owner of the garden, a white man, a missionary, gave him the vegetables to keep. But he also gave him some cards upon which were written Bible verses. "If you learn those verses," he said, "I will give you a pen." A great prize for a young man at Timbuktu. But with the learning of those precious words of scripture came not just a pen, but also the dawning light of conviction that these newly acquired words were true. As he learned more, the light of God shone into his soul.

But the words Nouh so eagerly continued to learn and his newfound faith brought shame and humiliation to the family. Their son had defiled their home. His talk of the Christian gospel put his very life in danger. And the threat became a dreadful reality when, because of the stand he took for Jesus, he was given a meal laced with deadly poison. He ate the food, but the wonder of his testimony is that it did him no harm. It paralyzed his brother with whom he shared it!

Determination and total commitment to live for Jesus have permeated Nouh's life. His strength, grace, and spirituality are rare and remarkable.

From the vantage point of the flat roof of Nouh's mud-brick home, so reminiscent of the homes of biblical days, we looked across that ancient city, with its aura of history and mystique. We spoke about his work as a pastor, as a shepherd to that tiny flock. "I am here," he said, "to love and to lead this small group of precious people." I asked him whether there were any secret believers among the rest of the population.

"You mean Nicodemuses?" he asked.

"There are many of them. They are secret disciples, who seek after Jesus, yet find it impossible to break with the cultural and social strength of Islam. I am here to care for and to love them as well."

He took us to a few huge "open" wells on the outskirts of the city. These wells of Timbuktu are not normal wells, small in diameter, from which water is winched to the surface in a bucket or other receptacle. Timbuktu's open wells resemble immense inverted conical pits, many hundreds of feet in diameter at the top, narrowing down to a small central hole in the bottom into which water seeps from an underground source. The pool of water at the bottom was brown and muddy.

Thousands of steps and small areas of garden were cut into the sloping walls of these deep conical pits. The well we visited was a hive of activity. Dozens of men and women, carrying buckets, pots, or skin receptacles, were continually running down the steps, collecting the precious water to carry it up to the small terraced gardens for which each of them was responsible. They were tending, with great care, various types of vegetables and edible plants, crucial for survival.

1987 was "survival time" in Timbuktu! Famine of devastating proportions had ravaged equatorial Africa from west to east. Tens of thousands had died, and millions more were under the threat of death, as seasonal rains yielded to the relentless sun that dried up the land. As in so many other natural disasters like this, the services of MAF were lifesaving. We provided transportation of relief supplies and gave mobility to the many people who came to help. It was a special privilege to be at the center of such an outpouring of compassion.

Our newfound pastor friend wanted Jo and me to go visit the cemetery at Timbuktu. Cemeteries are not usually on the "must do" list for us. But we acceded to his continuing request that we go there. I look back now upon that visit with profound gratitude for what I was about to see and experience.

The cemetery at Timbuktu was unlike any I had ever seen. There were no headstones, no identifying plaques. This was no lawn cemetery. Indeed, there were no real graves. It appeared akin to a place I knew only in the recesses of my imagination—the valley of dry bones—from Ezekiel 37. The scene was macabre. Bones, bleached by the burning sun, littered the entire area. Line after line of bare white skulls, each with a deathly grin, clearly marked the peculiar regimented rows of this strange, ancient graveyard.

The sands of the lower Sahara, like the dunes of a lonely foreshore, are constantly on the move, driven by strong, hot desert winds. Bodies buried beneath the sand soon, sometimes too soon, emerge from below to become skeletons littering the landscape of this burial ground.

Strangely, mixed with the regimented lines of bleached human remains were pieces of pottery. Some, on older graves, were small, crumbly orange-colored shards worn smooth by the relentless winds. On the newer graves, more gruesome-looking with their blowing remnants of shroud material slowly disintegrating in the scorching sun, the pottery pieces were sharper, newer, and larger. I could see they were the remnants of large water-pots, like those I'd seen in the houses of Timbuktu.

It was a strange and eerie place. Jo and I were deeply affected by the experience. We were aware at some indefinable level that there was a significant reason for us being there that day. As we walked through the lines of bones, I asked Nouh about the broken pottery pieces. He explained, "It is the custom of the people here, that when a body is buried, a pot is placed on the grave, then ceremonially broken to signify, with deep sadness, that, forever, life has drained away into the sand."

Standing there in a valley of dry bones, surrounded by the stark and chilling evidence of the hopelessness of death without Christ, we became poignantly aware of the presence of God to a degree we have seldom experienced. Passages from Scripture, some of them words of Jesus himself, came to my mind as if spoken by God himself.

"I, even I, am the Lord and apart from me there is no Savior."

"I am the way, the truth and the life. No man comes to the father but by me."

"He who hath the son hath life. He who hath not the Son of God hath not life. . . ."

It was a memorable experience. There was no "burning bush." There was no audible voice. But I felt we stood on holy ground, a place of profound challenge. We were in the company of this superb young man of Mali, a man of God. And God was there. In this remote desert cemetery, we felt him leading us, beckoning us on, challenging us to respond to this world of need where in so many places "life is draining away into the sand."

Later that day we drove out over the dunes of the Sahara to meet a group of people with whom Pastor Nouh was working. These were the legendary Berbers of the desert. Dignified and beautiful people, they carried an unmistakable air of nobility. I had read of their independence and their strength of character. They were cattle people of the desert. Their wealth had been in the herds of cattle and goats they drove from place to place in their nomadic wandering. But no cattle were left. Their goats had also been a traditional source of food and milk, their skins providing covering and protection. But there had been years of terrible drought. No goats were left. They had nothing. Now in the throws of famine, they were hanging on with desperation to the last vestiges of self-sufficiency and pride. They were hurting, disenfranchised, and on the brink of extinction. What is more, they seemed totally broken in spirit.

Now forced to abandon a nomadic way of life and settle in one place, they were enduring the ignominy of being "re-enculturated." They were learning how to garden, to grow food in the ground, and to stay there long enough for it to produce. As a part of the international effort and outpouring of compassion for Mali's suffering, a deep-shaft well had been dug for them from which they were able to draw water for their small, square garden plots in the sand. As they poured this meager water supply from the goatskin buckets onto the rows of little plants, patting up the sandy sides of each area so the water couldn't escape, they looked more like sad children playing games on a seaside beach than noble cattlemen of the desert.

It was a heart-wrenching sight. Hungry, pitifully thin, they were wrapped in dark desert robes. I could only see black hands, faces, and piercing black eyes. Their long-term survival seemed unlikely.

The women and children were sitting in the shade of inadequate shelters, skin-covered framework of sticks providing little protection from the blistering rays of the sun. I felt an overwhelming sense of frustration that I, personally, could do so little for them on that day. We gave them the grain we had brought in the truck, but that was barely a short-term solution. What would their tomorrow bring? With a troubled heart I walked alone around those simple huts.

Looking into these eyes filled with overwhelming sadness and hopelessness, I understood why my staff, even the tough ones, in their reports back to my office had spoken so often of their own tears and of the almost unbearable emotional pressure of working among these people.

I found myself humming a little song. My surprise was not that I was humming. I often do that. It was rather the particular song that had subconsciously come to my mind. Just as the bones and the pottery of the morning's visit to the cemetery had been used to speak to me a profound message, so did this little song in the afternoon hours in that heart-breaking environment of thirst and death.

> I've got a river of life flowing out of me,
>> makes the lame to walk and the blind to see,
> opens prison doors, sets the captives free,
>> I've got a river of life flowing out of me.

These people desperately needed the generous help of overseas governments and aid organizations in digging wells and sending other assistance. They needed even their impossible dream of another breed of cattle able to survive the rigors of the Sahara Desert that could return their culture to them. They needed the grain we carried. They needed loving hands to dispense those life-saving things.

"I've got a river of life flowing out of me."

More than anything else they needed that "stream of living water" that Jesus says flows from the innermost being of those who truly believe in him.

That "living water" is ours to give.

Timbuktu. What a name. It is not an imaginary place, a fantasy in a small boy's storybook. It is a wonderful, unique, ancient city of rich culture—and the parish of one of the finest young men I have ever met. ★

Chapter Fourteen

··· An Albanian Named Jimmy ···

So from Jerusalem all the way round to Illyricum, I have fully proclaimed the gospel of Christ. It has always been my ambition to preach the gospel where Christ was not known.

ROMANS 15:19–20

"Jimmy" was from Albania. To this day, I don't know his real name. He told me one day, but he laughed as I tried to pronounce it. "Forget it," he said. "It's an Albanian name. Anything to do with Albania only brings sadness and pain. Just call me Jimmy."

So Jimmy he was. And I loved him.

The year was 1977. We met in an orthopedic ward of a Melbourne hospital. Both of us were trussed up like chickens at the time in "seven-pound traction," a sadistically designed instrument of torture for the treatment for the spinal disk problem we each had. Heavy weights attached to our legs with an apparatus of cords and pulleys were intended to "stretch" us back into shape! So there we lay, captive audience to one another. For hours we talked, often through the long hours of the night, sharing stories.

It was hard to believe the things he told me about Albania. My knowledge of his strange and secretive homeland was very scanty. I knew that Russia had been considered too liberal for the Albanian leadership, which then made friends with China. It had been the only nation in the world to declare itself atheistic and was brutal to any of its citizens who broke the laws banning religion.

Jimmy's life in Albania had left scars on his heart. Nevertheless, he had probably been as much a problem to the authorities as they had been to him. He was a "loveable rascal" with a twinkle in his eye! He wrought havoc among the nurses, indiscreetly taunting and provoking them. They scolded him continuously, often with blushes of embarrassment at his jokes and language, which were colorful to say the least. He had acquired his English in a decidedly rough and uncouth environment. But those nurses loved him as much as I did.

There was no twinkle in his eye, however, when he told me of his last night in Albania. He described how he had gone down to the beach, looked back at the land of his birth, and muttered to himself, "I would rather die than stay here." And taking off his clothes, he had swum out into the ocean in the darkness.

But Jimmy found freedom the next day. Some distance out on the Adriatic and clinging to a length of floating timber, he was rescued by the crew of an Italian fishing boat. He claimed asylum in Italy and, in time, began a new life in Australia as a political refugee.

Jimmy, in the dark of night, sometimes cried.

I longed to introduce him to Jesus. Occasionally, I read to him from the Bible. And sometimes he would shed tears of gratitude when I prayed for him, for his land, and his people.

I never led him to Christ. Yielding didn't come easily to him. And eventually I was released from the hospital. When I returned, as soon as I was able to visit him, I found that he too had been discharged—and was gone. I traced his address and went there, hoping to find him. He had disappeared.

I never saw Jimmy again.

Many times since over the years, I have thought about him. I have often found myself driving by the simple rooming house in Melbourne where he had lived. I have prayed, as I do still, that wherever Jimmy is, God would protect my dear friend. And perhaps lead him to that place where there is to be no more tears.

Jimmy left me a legacy of love. A love for him and for his homeland. That strange Balkan nation had somehow become very significant in my heart and thinking, although my faith was too small to even imagine that I would ever visit there. It was a closed and mysterious country.

Eventually, however, things changed. In 1985, Enver Hoxha, Albania's communist dictator, died. Control passed into other hands, equally as hard. They too ruled with iron fists and kept the doors firmly shut to the outside world. But the world, and even Albania, was changing.

Sitting at my desk in Redlands, California, my thoughts often turned to Albania. It remained separated from the rest of the world behind walls of oppression and godlessness. I prayed for the people, as I had done many times, that they someday would have the opportunity in freedom and openness to learn about the God who loved them. I took a file from my drawer. The tab said "Albania." I read again the material I had gathered over the years and placed it back in the cabinet under *A*.

In the early nineties, what had seemed entirely impossible became reality! The dividing wall had come down in Germany. The USSR had begun to crumble. Totalitarian communism was dying. And its demise was heralded the threshold to freedom for the people of those ancient lands struggling to loosen their bonds and begin a new way of life.

The domino effect was sweeping and immediate. Freedom was even on the horizon for Albania. And in that ancient land, known in Bible times as Illyricum, the ancient door began to creak open.

Then one day in 1990 as I prayed, with my now fat Albania file open before me on my desk, the phone rang.

It was a man totally unknown to me. But he was calling to ask whether I would consider being a part of a small delegation. A delegation to enter Albania! Of all places.

Because of other commitments, and much to my disappointment, I had to send someone else. Yet as a result of that visit, MAF-USA became a leading player, from the outset, in the establishment of the new evangelistic thrust in that Balkan nation.

And when finally, in 1991, I descended the steps of a Swiss-Air DC-9 and stepped onto Albanian soil, it was a moment of profound joy and poignant memory. Jimmy's homeland.

"Anything to declare?" This familiar question came not from a sophisticated customs officer but from a rather diminutive middle-aged lady dressed in an oversized khaki-colored army greatcoat buttoned up to the neck. The red star on her cap needed a polish.

"No," I said as I walked by her. I had nothing to declare.

My first impression of Albania was of the tangible fear under which its people lived. Thousands of dome-shaped concrete bunkers, gun emplacements, were randomly positioned along the roadside, like giant mushrooms in the fields. They were even between houses. Now empty, they had once been occupied by conscripted militiamen who had lived an abiding but deliberately perpetrated fear that "the Americans were coming to destroy them!"

As I stood on the roof of the Tirana hotel at 6:00 A.M. the following morning, I looked down upon the city square. Thousands of people made their way to work. All I could hear was the slapping sound of shoes against the pavement, but no other noise. There were no vehicles. Not even the sound of soft human voices drifting up to me from below. Just the sound of people walking.

Albanians didn't talk to strangers. People were not to be trusted.

In the depth of the soul of this people was a vast, deep void. And it was strangely familiar. Something was missing. I had seen it before . . . all those years ago, in a Melbourne hospital room.

But fear was in retreat in Albania. The sense of anticipation and hope was unmistakable. A new wind was blowing. A new light was dawning upon the nation's darkened soul. On the day before my arrival in Tirana, thousands of angry but triumphant students had toppled the statue of Enver Hoxha that had stood for generations in the city square.

The air of triumph was most manifest at the "Freedom Concert" I attended in Tirana's city hall. The roar of applause from the mainly student audience was electrifying as they yelled their appreciation and expressed their national pride as they listened to the old Albanian folk songs and watched the dances. There were many tears of joy in that place that night. Sitting through that superb concert, I felt almost like an intruder. The night belonged to Albania, to Albanians, not to casual visitors from the West to enjoy. The night belonged to Jimmy. I wished he had been there with me.

On a visit to Skodra, Albania's northernmost city, I met a man who was exactly my age. We had been born within a few days of each other in 1935. Our lives, however, had been lived in vastly different ways. I thought about my life of freedom, of ease and comfort, of travel and excitement as he told me about his. He had been put into prison with his entire aristocratic family when he was nine years old! Nine years old! For almost forty-seven years he had been deprived of basic personal freedom. Upon his release, just a short time before our arrival, what remained of his old family estate had been returned to him.

So I visited this man in his once-magnificent mansion. It was now almost lost in the mass of crudely constructed high-density housing pressing right up against its walls. A beautiful mosaic sidewalk created by a master craftsman more than a century ago and which had formally meandered through the expansive grounds and gardens, was barely discernable in a few places between the masses of rundown dwellings. As this man, the grandson of a former prince of the Balkans, sat in one of the only two habitable rooms of that grand old home, he said, with no sign of emotion whatsoever, "And now I am free."

It seemed as if the ability to understand or express the concept of freedom had been lost behind all the razor wire of forty-seven years.

Jimmy had achieved freedom by placing his life at risk. This man had been finally granted his freedom. But for both Jimmy and this aristocratic man of Skodra, there was another kind of freedom. It was a freedom about which neither of them knew anything at all.

And as I had told Jimmy in that hospital bed so many years before, I again struggled to tell this man in Skodra about that other freedom available to him, the freedom of the soul. Spiritual freedom. That spiritual freedom is not achieved by risking one's life, or by swimming into the darkness, or even by the opening of prison gates. This freedom is lasting and indestructible. And it is available to all who will accept it, through the One who gently and lovingly says, "If the son shall make you free, you shall be free indeed."

In 1990, we knew of only about thirty Christians in Albania. But the beginnings of spiritual freedom were evident nonetheless. Deeply dedicated people were coming from all points of the globe to share God's love. I went to church in the sitting room of an old stone house not far from the center of Tirana.

There was no notice board, no stained glass, very little furniture, no pulpit. There were no well-dressed people there. There was no church bulletin and no ordained preacher. A young, Italian-speaking man from Switzerland in his early twenties was their pastor.

These Albanian Christ-followers didn't know how to "do church!" These were people who were just passionately in love with Jesus! And there, I saw "joy unspeakable." This joy lit up the faces of the few Albanians who were there in a way I had never seen. As they worshiped, I was brought to tears.

God had not abandoned these people. No godless dictator and his evil regime had eradicated God from this nation. Perhaps one might say Hoxha was almost successful. Yes, there was little understanding of God's love in Albania in those early nineties. Only the old could remember. Anyone younger than forty-seven years would only have been told of God in absolute secrecy. It seemed as if the very soul of the nation had been taken almost to the brink of destruction.

But only to the brink!

A couple of times I sat in the lobby of the Hotel Tirana and made sure there was an empty chair by my side. Within minutes, someone would come and ask, with typical Albanian courtesy, "May I sit by you?"

Then, every time, the same questions would come. Phrased differently? Perhaps. But the same. A longing of soul.

"Are you from the West?"

"May I speak with you about life outside Albania?"

"Who is God? Is he real? Does he really care about us? Is there any hope? What is the church? Can it help us find a new dignity?"

As I was driven to Tirana's international airport some days later, I remembered the khaki-coated lady who had greeted me upon arrival. I could still hear her question, "Anything to declare?"

I looked for her but couldn't find her. I wanted to tell her, "Yes! Yes! I do have something to declare!" This was no trite item that would attract duty! This was without price but beyond value. And I longed to tell her.

The Psalmist tells us, "Declare his glory among the nations, his marvelous deeds among all peoples." That is the declaration we make to the nation of Albania.

Since those early days, the people of God from the free world have with great clarity and effectiveness made that declaration in Albania.

Today, there are not so many foreigners in Albania. It's a good thing. The new Albanian church that came to birth in the agony of a disenfranchised and oppressed people is strong. It is withstanding the predictable pressure of entry into the world of capitalism. It doesn't need so many outsiders now. Predictably, some new believers have drifted away, but there are thousands who remain firm in their newfound faith.

I visited Albania again in June 1999, this time at the invitation of the association of evangelical churches. In 1990 there were less than fifty believers there. Nine years later I spoke to pastors and leaders representing more than 160 churches.

The touch of God has been upon that land in the decade of the nineties. Miracles have happened. Lives have been transformed. People have been empowered as a church has been born. It is a church that, though young in experience and in years, is vitally alive and gloriously enthusiastic. The experience of hearing them sing, of sensing their joy, and feeling their irrepressible spirit will remain one of the highlights of my life.

At the time of my visit in 1999, Albania was caught in the midst of the terrible ethnic and cultural crisis between the Serbs of Yugoslavia and the ethnic Albanians of Kosovo. More than four hundred thousand ethnic Albanians had fled south from Kosovo to Albania, seeking safety. Refugee camps were established all over the country, some as "tent cities" in the countryside, some occupying long-derelict buildings in Albanian towns and cities. Kosovar lives had been shattered as the Yugoslavian military seemed to have been given the freedom to do their worst among them. Stories of ethnic cleansing, of rape, pillage, and murder were rife among these refugee people.

International relief agencies flooded into Albania. The international airport looked like a war zone with aircraft of all shapes and sizes crowding its tarmac and aprons. Military forces from major European nations and the U.S. built their own tent cities in the area. Large transport aircraft brought food and other material aid to these deprived and disenfranchised refugees. At night the noise of high flying NATO fighter planes and bombers was a constant drone as they flew across Albania to drop their destructive payloads on Yugoslavian targets.

And where was this young, enthusiastic Albanian church at this time of pressure and tension?

The church was in the refugee camps, ministering to the grieving, to the lost, to the hurting ethnic Albanians of Kosovo who had come seeking refuge. Along with food, clothing, and encouragement, these refugees from the north who were mainly Muslim in faith received the Good News of Jesus Christ! Muslim refugees, astounded at the love shown by their Albanian Christian brothers and sisters, flocked into the churches of Albania. They could not believe that people could be so loving, so caring.

Church leaders were making plans, deciding which of their people would go with the refugees back to Kosovo when they were able to return home. These new relationships were seen as a God-given challenge to continue to share their faith with the Kosavars—in Kosovo. This was to be their first missionary endeavor—and they were not going to miss the opportunity. God's opportunity.

The nurses in the Mitcham Private Hospital in Melbourne would never agree, but I think, in a way, Jimmy was a kind of angel! He came into my life just for three short weeks. But he was used of God to open my mind and prepare me for an appointment some fourteen years later. Through a trussed-up friend, carrying a heart full of pain, God planted a seed that would spring to life and bear much fruit.

Makes you think about "casual" acquaintances, doesn't it?

I wish I knew where Jimmy was today. ✸

PART FOUR

Chapter Fifteen

··· Boyhood ···

You created my inmost being; you knit me together in my mother's womb. . . . My frame was not hidden from you when I was made in the secret place. When I was woven together in the depths of the earth, your eyes saw my unformed body. All the days ordained for me were written in your book before one of them came to be.

PSALM 139:13, 15–16

My happiest memories of schooldays are of playing hookey! "Wagging it," we used to say.

It was tantamount to bliss, stretching out on the hot, golden sands on a beautiful Sydney beach with a couple of mates, chuckling at the thought of the rest of our class crowded into a stuffy schoolroom, laboring over the declension of a complicated Latin verb or agonizing through a complex algebraic equation. The sapphire sea, the soft, yellow sand, and the crashing of the surf were far better than the dull walls and the droning voice of a ho-hum teacher. These were days of boyhood triumph. The system could be challenged and beaten. Or so I thought at the time.

While school could occasionally be fun, for the most part, to me it was more like a kind of prison. I was smart. I did well, when I worked at it. An incessant monotonous "sameness." How I longed to escape, to launch out, to be different, to embrace a future in which things were not always done in the same predictable way. So as a boy I would dream. And voraciously read any story of adventure I could lay my hands on. I dreamed of travel to faraway places. And of flying.

While not on the best of speaking terms with God, I used to pray that things would change for me. But I couldn't see how.

World War II was in full swing. A fascination with airplanes was a driving force in my life. All the kids in our street could readily identify them . . . a Spitfire, a Hurricane, a Liberator, a Mitchell, a Flying Fortress, a Dakota, or a Mustang. More than a childhood dream, airplanes became a passion through those growing years.

To fly was to be my escape route. My path upward and outward!

VP day, August 15, 1945, was a wild and memorable occasion. "Victory in the Pacific." The skies above Sydney were swamped with airplanes as Air Force pilots celebrated with grand, exuberant aerial dances.

Standing in the center of the road, I traced with wide-eyed boyish wonder a lone U.S. Air Force "Thunderbolt" fighter, weaving its magic overhead. Then, all of a sudden, with a deafening roar, it flew right down our street. I could barely contain my excitement. I waved excitedly and leaped up and down. It was right there. So close. I could almost reach out and touch it. The pilot, having slid open the canopy, was clearly visible. I could see his grinning face! And as he swept by, he looked down at a little boy with dreams in his heart, waving and leaping exuberantly. He circled around and repeated the performance, this time so low that I thought he would hit the light poles that lined the street.

He waved and rocked his wings, just for me, as he flew away.

It was clear. And it was settled. Once and for all. I had to fly!

To be born into a churchgoing family was no sign of fortune's favor. Not, at least, from my perspective.

While the things of God were not talked of much at home, there was no doubt where my mom and dad stood as far as faith was concerned. They were different. Church every Sunday. Grace at the table. Prayers at night. Strong rules and guidelines. And Sundays were tough. It was embarrassing for a boy! Not only were we dressed and polished for church, but we then had to walk off to the bus stop, together. As a family. When most of the other boys in the street had the day to play.

But my parents built a heritage for me that became more meaningful as the years passed by. Even to this day, when I am enveloped in an atmosphere of pure worship, be it in a church or in private, when the presence of God is so real, I find myself worshiping with my hands together, palm to palm, in front of my face. Like a little child. It's the way I was taught to pray. And I am taken back to that childhood in worship. A precious heritage! My mom and dad may not have been overtly expressive, but by their lifestyle, their teaching, and their modeling, they pointed my eyes toward God from the very beginning.

One church service in those early forties stands crystal clear in my memory. A visiting American preacher named George Fisk kept the congregation spellbound as he told of his missionary work on the island of Borneo. He told tales of impenetrable jungles and difficult journeys along raging rivers to reach the Dyaks, the "Headhunters of Borneo," with the gospel. He talked of those wild people "giving their hearts to Jesus."

He spoke of being on one such river journey and dragging a long canoe over the rocks of a remote rapid. He turned his gaze skywards. He eyed the birds winging their way effortlessly overhead and dreamed of a day when he, too, would fly over the jungles.

Why can't I fly? he thought. He went on to recount his subsequent purchase and use of a Beechcraft "Stagger-wing" aircraft in the next years of his gospel work.

As I listened to him speak—I was there. I was with him. In my mind I, too, was skimming those treetops too. My question echoed his: "Why can't I fly?"

But the "giving my heart to Jesus" bit was another matter altogether. In fact, it was the last thing I wanted to do. My heart belonged to me. Why should I give it away?

But as time passed, an inner voice seemed to be saying to me, with increasing frequency and intensity, "I understand you. I know about you, your dreams of flying, your reluctance to follow me. Max, I like what I see in you, and I love you deeply." God was not chasing me after all, I realized, but beckoning with love.

He didn't really want my ambition. He wanted me!

There was a lady named Mrs. Harrison who came to church every Sunday. Dressed in black. We liked Mrs. Harrison so much because after church she would open her large, black handbag and give each of the kids a piece of very sweet, boiled candy. We liked her, as well, because she was genuinely interested in us.

"Max, what do you want to do when you grow up?" She asked me one day.

"I want to fly!"

She turned aside for a minute and said "I don't know too many verses in the Bible that speak about flying, but here's one. It comes from the book of Deuteronomy. She then read out loud to me, "There is no one like the God of Jeshurun, who rides on the heavens to help you and on the clouds in his majesty. The eternal God is your refuge, and underneath are the everlasting arms."

"I think God knows all about flying," Mrs. Harrison said. "He rides on the heavens to help you." That verse and the memory of that wonderful old lady have never left me.

My first outward response to God's voice was at a Communion service. In our little church, Communion services were for adults only and were tacked on to the end of the Sunday morning services. Communion to me had always meant an extra fifteen minutes of boredom. This one, however, was different. A departure from routine. It was for a group of teenagers. These kids acted and spoke as if they really knew God personally. I was confused . . . because I had always associated a relationship with God with adults, with the pastor, my parents, and their friends.

Whatever it was that these kids had, I found myself wanting it.

As I took that small piece of bread and, then, a tiny glass of grape juice, I felt that in that crowded little room God and I were there alone. Even though I felt guilty and a little afraid, I was certain of his presence. I could feel it. And I yielded to this loving, caring God.

More years passed. There was another life-altering church service in 1950. I was sitting with my friends in the back row, as usual, expecting nothing spectacular. Simply passing time. A very attractive young couple walked into the church. Total strangers. The secretary began the announcements in his usual sonorous tone. He welcomed the two visitors, Mr. and Mrs. Hutchins, and explained that they were missionaries. We boys thought that she was too pretty to be a missionary.

"Mr. Hutchins plans to be a different kind of missionary," the church secretary went on. "He is a pilot. And he's in Australia for a short while before going to New Guinea with a new organization called Missionary Aviation Fellowship. His flying across the jungles of New Guinea will be a lifeline for missionaries who work in the remote places of that land."

I was captivated. I remembered back to that American, George Fisk.

I didn't have the courage to speak with Bob and Betty Hutchins, but thirty years later, in their home in the U.S., I shared with them how their coming to our church was a life-changing event in my young life. I would never have imagined that, as the president of that same MAF, I would speak at their retirement dinner in California in 1991, privileged to honor their forty years of committed service.

And so as childhood gave way to adolescence, I somehow knew that I was "sought after," found, was being changed, and that something wonderful lay ahead for me as a follower of Jesus . . . and as a pilot.

At sixteen years of age I would walk across the tarmac at Bankstown airport in Sydney to take my first flying lesson. It was a pre-World War II DeHavilland DH82 "Tiger Moth" in which I learned to fly. I knew by then, with absolute certainty, that God's call upon my life was to serve in missions. Leaving school at fifteen, I had worked full time to pay for these flying lessons. Then, at eighteen, having completed the training for a commercial pilots license, I embarked on a further seven years of MAF preparation by becoming a pilot in the Royal Australian Air Force. Another story!

In 1961, with the resignation of my Air Force commission behind me, I found myself on the way to Papua New Guinea with Jo and the eldest of our sons, Michael.

Childhood. Wonderful memories.

But it is more than memories. Looking back, I see a record of God's involvement in a life he designed, made . . . and loved.

It is simply impossible for me to look back over my childhood and say that those things "just happened." I would rather agree with King David who said, "all the days ordained for me were written in [God's] book before one of them came to be." ✸

Chapter Sixteen

··· The Lostness of the Lost ···

Suppose one of you has a hundred sheep and loses one of them. Does he not leave the ninety-nine in the open country and go after the lost sheep until he finds it? And when he finds it, he joyfully puts it on his shoulders and goes home. Then he calls his friends and neighbors together and says, "Rejoice with me; I have found my lost sheep."

LUKE 15:3–6

It was the greatest show on earth. But it was no three-ringed circus. It would have been an international blockbuster, but no Broadway or Hollywood producer could have put this show together. Its cast of tens of thousands was totally untrained. Yet each one knew his role before the show was ever envisaged. There were no rehearsals. There was no program. There were no lights, no sound system. No tickets. There was not even an audience! The set was magnificent and unique. No artist could ever have painted that mountain backdrop. It was indeed like no other show on earth—ever.

And it was a stunning success!

It was called, simply, the Mount Hagen Show.

It was a gathering together of warriors from the mountains and valleys of the western and southern highlands of Papua New Guinea. For some years there had been a smaller annual show, or "sing-sing," at Mount Hagen to which the people of the Whagi and other nearby valleys had been invited. But this year, 1965, tribes from hundreds of miles away had been invited to come as well. From villages and hamlets

123

perched precariously on the sides of steep, spectacular mountains. From faraway valleys. This was to be a coming together of people who had never met, indeed whose awareness and knowledge of each other was very scanty. Most of these men had never seen a town—or a car. They were wild and exotic people. This show was for them and for them alone.

Inviting them to gather at Mount Hagen was a part of the government's strategy to unify a deeply divided people. It was part of the plan to make one nation out of hundreds of different tribal and cultural groups. Seven hundred fifty languages! A gargantuan task.

To an outsider these men, with their common Melanesian features, may have looked the same, but the subcultures among them were profoundly diverse. Bringing them together might help them see that despite the unique differences between their tribes, they had great and unifying commonalities. This gathering was to facilitate their ultimate unification as one people to take their place among the nations of the world with dignity and pride.

The entire concept was considered by some to be reckless in the extreme, an invitation to riot and debacle. But it was going to be exciting!

By messages shouted from ridge to ridge across that rugged land and carried on foot across the mountains, the word was sent out. "There is going to be a 'bigpela sing-sing' at Mount Hagen." Boundaries, sacred and sacrosanct, were to be lifted to allow free travel for all, even sworn enemies, to make their way there.

This show was the main topic of conversation all over the highland regions. I was asked about it at every airstrip. Excitement mounted, and a sense of eager anticipation was everywhere.

As the day grew closer, groups of colorful men from faraway valleys began the long walk to Mount Hagen. They marched with pride through "enemy" territory, challenging any authority who tried to stop this granted free passage. As they walked, they sang a strange chant-like cadence.

Bodies were greased to a bright sheen with pig fat and tree oil. An amazing array of brightly colored feather headdresses, made from the dried carcasses of birds of paradise, marked these men as unique among world citizens. The vivid brilliance of these tall, waving crowns of glory was in stark contrast to the charcoal-blackened faces and the circles of white ochre ringing the eyes of the proud wearers.

They held their weapons high, these highland men. And with great pride. Long spears of polished black palm, bows with arrows intricately carved and tipped with wicked-looking sharpened bone. In each bark belt was a traditional stone ax, the blades hewn from mountain rock, patiently and meticulously ground to the traditional shape and sharp edge.

Standing on the porch of our house at Wapenamanda, watching these men pass by on their long walk to Mount Hagen, I pictured thousands of them all in one place at the one time. It was going to be an incredible spectacle, a historic occasion. It was not to be missed. I simply couldn't stay away.

At the last moment I decided to take our second son, three-year-old Tim, with me. It was to be a special day out with Dad for him. It proved to be special in an entirely different way.

We flew the twenty minutes to the Mount Hagen airstrip and walked the mile or so to the large area of level valley land set aside for the show. By the time we arrived, dust was swirling and rising from tens of thousands of feet as these magnificent highlanders leapt and danced their way in a strange circling movement around the arena. Their intriguing singing was, to the uninitiated, more akin to yelling. An unusual cacophony of sound. The air was electric.

As some had predicted, there was a fine line between spectacle and danger. The spears, arrows, and stone axes brandished by these fighting men were not toy weapons. These were the weapons of war and of death. These were men of war and of death.

With Tim on my shoulders, I approached the split-bamboo fence roughly erected a few days before and now encircling a solid mass of human bodies. Tim's little knees tightened against my neck. He grasped two fistfuls of my hair, far too tight for comfort. His excitement rapidly became apprehension.

Entering the enclosure we joined the crowd, or more realistically, we were simply absorbed into a maelstrom of people. There was nothing else we could do. It was not a matter of moving around from group to group. The many thousands moved as one, like a massive, brown, human whirlpool, rotating in slow motion. It was impossible to walk against the flow. All around us, shoulder to shoulder, were men, not simply of another culture, but of another age. The smell of sweaty bodies, of tree oil, and pig fat was almost overpowering.

The noise was deafening. Every warrior was singing the high-pitched yelling chants unique to his own tribe.

And in the middle of this incredible spectacle, perched high on my shoulders, my small, snowy-haired, pale-skinned boy—dressed so neatly in white overalls and matching hat by his mother for this special day—was very uncomfortable. And increasingly afraid. He was constantly being brushed in the face with feathered headdresses and had to push aside bows, arrows, and spears. He cried for me to let him down. I carried him in my arms for a while, but he then found himself bumping not against feathers and weapons but against strong, sweaty, greasy bodies.

It didn't take long to decide that one circuit of that large arena would be enough. This was no place for a little boy.

I tried to stand still but the crowd pressed us on. I lifted Tim down to the ground, and holding his little hand firmly, I tried to work my way to the periphery of the arena.

Perhaps he needed to wipe his eyes; perhaps it was because our hands had become oily and greasy we were pulled apart. I don't know. I just know that, in an instant, his little hand was jerked from mine.

He was gone, lost in that crowd. Danger. Extreme danger. And I could do nothing about it.

I yelled for people to get out of the way to let me find my son. I pushed my way back through the press of brown, gyrating bodies to where we had been when our hands slipped apart. Not finding him, I forced my way forward, then back against that milling crowd—but he was nowhere to be seen. I elbowed my way toward the center of the circle then back again, yelling his name continually. But it was all to no avail. My voice was lost in the noise of that place. A little boy three feet high was not to be easily seen, nor his voice heard.

Fear, abject fear, exploded throughout my entire being. I had lost my son in that seething mass of humanity, in that hostile and dangerous place. I fell to my knees in an attempt to see him among the impenetrable barrier of dark, dusty, dancing legs, appalled at the thought that he could be so easily trampled underfoot.

Guilt flooded over me. What a stupid and irresponsible thing I had done in bringing him here. I should have never put him down to the ground—or let him go.

In this very, very dangerous place I found it hard to control panic.

There was no office to which I could go to report him missing. My frantic shouts drew no attention. Tens of thousands of others were also shouting. Very few could even understand my language or my pleas for help. The occasional English-speaking foreigner who came by could do little but shrug his shoulders. They were sympathetic but soon were forced to pass on. I didn't know whether to move along with the crowd or to remain in one spot.

I felt paralyzed with helplessness.

The minutes stretched on. It seemed that for hours I struggled from place to place trying to find someone who could help in my attempts to locate my son. I found one government officer, but there was little he could do.

I cried out, with deep emotion, to God, "Please, please, help me find my son. Please protect him. Please keep him safe in this incredibly dangerous place. Please."

I have no idea of the duration of time of my total despair. Perhaps it was only thirty minutes. It felt like many hours.

With an increasing sense of doom I worked my way to the edge of the crowd. There was rising ground there. I had made a full circle of that vast area. Climbing the flattened grass of that little hill with a heavy, heavy heart, I was physically and emotionally drained, completely exhausted.

But as I walked up the slope, overwhelmed by dejection and loss, I saw a little white boy at the edge of the crowd, standing by the bamboo wall. With him was a Papua New Guinean boy just a few years older.

Tim!

He threw himself into my arms, gripping me with all of his remaining strength. Totally disheveled, his once clean outfit was brown with dirt and grease, his little white hat long since gone, no doubt by now trampled into a small, unrecognizable piece of dirty ragged cloth. His face was streaked with the dried mud of tears mixed with dust. He buried his head into my neck and, with a hoarse, exhausted voice, sobbed into my ear, "Daddy, Daddy, I was . . . been . . . trying to find you."

I sobbed with him. For several minutes I clung to him as if I would never let him go again. My tears were of indescribable joy, my sobs of deep relief. My precious little son was found. I stood there, profoundly thankful to God for answered prayer.

Only then did I turn to the small Papua New Guinean boy. I looked down at him as he stood there by me with a wide smile on his face—a warrior in miniature. His joy was obvious as he saw the little white-skinned boy he had rescued reunited with his father. His little body shone with fat and oil. He carried his weapons and his little stone ax with pride. His feathers were beautiful, his face blackened with charcoal.

I lifted him with my other arm and held him close, sharing my tears of relief with him. He didn't understand the words of my outpoured feelings of gratitude as I told him over and over again how much I loved him for what he had done. I owed the life of my son to him, but I didn't know how to express it, how to repay him.

Eventually I put him down and, emptying my pockets, gave him all the money I had. It seemed such a paltry reward. He had given up participating in what was to him an unbelievably exciting thing to help a distressed little white boy.

But he soon rushed off into the crowd, and I have never seen him again. I have often wondered what happened to him. Did he grow up to be a proud village warrior? Was he one, who, as development and independence finally came to Papua New Guinea, achieved great things in the leadership of his people? I don't know. But I do know that he meant more to me that day than I could possibly have told him.

I took Tim "far from that madding crowd." We finished our special day in relative quietness and arrived home hours earlier than we had anticipated.

The "lostness of the lost." What does this mean . . . to you? What does it mean to God?

That day has become for me an unforgettable benchmark against which I regularly and with great seriousness measure my own life. Even today, as I relive the anguish of that hour and then its wonderful conclusion, things come to mind that are of momentous importance.

The analogy, the parable, fails in some respects, but in others it is potent and telling. If, as an imperfect human parent, I could feel the depth of emotion and passion that was mine that day, if "separation and lostness" produce such an overwhelming sense of love and concern—and if God is truly our Father—how does he feel about the lost of this world?

The Scriptures clearly tell us "your father in heaven is not willing that any of these little ones should be lost."

Jesus, in the parable of the lost sheep, made it abundantly clear that finding his lost children is paramount to the Father. The shepherd's responsibility demands that he leave the ninety-nine to seek and save one that is lost.

A final thought. As I think of that young boy from Papua New Guinea, as I recall my deep love and gratitude to him, I am reminded also of another great and wonderful truth.

The Father has a special measure of love for those who bring the lost back to him. ✸

Chapter Seventeen

··· The Invisible Communion ···

I pray also for those who will believe in me . . . that all of them may be one, Father, just as you are in me and I am in you."

JOHN 17:20–21

I have a vivid boyhood memory of a photograph taken during the blitz of London in World War II. It was a stark black-and-white photo of the dome of St. Paul's Cathedral silhouetted against the brilliant yet awful light of a hundred surrounding fires. Wave after wave of German bombers had dropped tons of bombs on London. Yet, miraculously, St. Paul's stood, miraculously untouched, through it all.

One summer day I went to St. Paul's with a good friend. It seemed more like a tourist attraction than a church. We ducked and weaved our way up the steps through a crowd of visitors, all wanting to take in the wonder of this architectural phenomenon. It was more like a market than a church. People were talking loudly in any of a dozen languages. Some were buying gifts at a store to the side. Others dropped coins into a receptacle, making perfunctory donations toward immense maintenance costs.

St. Paul's Cathedral is a church, a house of God. It was designed and built for worship. At various times during the week and on Sunday, genuine and reverent believers meet there. But that day there was no sense of worship at all. I think the crowd at the British Museum and the National Gallery not far away would have been more quiet and respectful.

At 12:15, a black-robed priest appeared. He made his way through the crowd and climbed the shiny brass spiral staircase to the pulpit. Standing behind a magnificent polished brass eagle whose wings formed the base of the lectern, he switched on the public address system and, in a cultured English voice, made his announcement, "There will be a service of Holy Communion in the chapel on my right beginning at 12:30. We warmly invite you to join us." This was what we had been waiting for.

There was momentary silence as the priest began to speak, but very quickly the hum of conversation and cacophony of sound returned. Who cared for a noon-hour Communion service?

Seventeen people waited in the exquisite chapel to the side. The priest, now in the dignified and colorful vestments that marked his office, warmly welcomed us and with a prayer of invocation began the service of Communion:

"The Lord Jesus, on the night he was betrayed, took bread, and when he had blessed it he said, 'This is my body, which is for you. Do this in remembrance of me.' In the same way he took the cup, saying, 'This cup is the new covenant in my blood; do this whenever you drink it, in memory of me.'"

We went forward to the altar to receive the elements. It was a special time of worship, thirty minutes of rich and deep blessing. The world outside, in the hallowed sanctuary, continued on, noisily unaware.

Only seventeen. For me at that Wednesday noon-hour, St. Paul's Cathedral took on a new meaning. It was a true cathedral, a house of God. No longer a tourist attraction. Though not set against the glow of a hundred war-fires, it glowed for me that day. And for sixteen others.

We were a diverse group, probably from many parts of the world. But we were drawn together by a bond. And we were one.

Another time, another place. . . .

Guatemala looked beautiful. Majestic mountains and rolling hills stood in brilliant contrast to the green cultivated valleys and to the sophisticated cities of the south.

"What's that little place down there?' I asked Ludin, the pilot. We were en route from Coban to Barrillas in a small MAF airplane. Below, adjacent to a small village, a roughly constructed airstrip looked like a scar in the jungle. "It's called Mayaland," Ludin replied. "There's rebel activity in the area. The military has virtually taken over the village, making the people feel almost like intruders in their own homes. There is a strong church there, but the people are living under a lot of pressure at present."

Our work for the day was done so we decided to pay them a visit.

"These are Mayan people," Ludin explained as we taxied toward the parking bay. "Their ancestors were the ones who built the ancient pyramids. Those ruins are our greatest tourist attraction."

As the propeller jerked to a stop, a crowd of armed and uniformed soldiers immediately swarmed around the airplane. They came down from the village mainly out of curiosity, to see who it was that had made this unscheduled landing. We told them we had come to visit the people of the village. They lost interest and began to wander away. "They are down there," the officer among them indicated, pointing toward the thick jungle. "They are in their church, I think."

And what a church it was! It looked as if it were made of firewood. It seemed that the walls, which were simple, rough-hewn vertical lengths of jungle timber, could scarcely hold up the roof. Even the woven grass thatch was sparse.

The people were there in the church, about thirty in number. Simple, peasant farmers of Guatemala, they were surprised and delighted to see their friend Ludin. They had thought the airplane they had heard was on a military supply trip. They greeted me also, with genuine warmth and pleasure. Their faces beamed.

No beautifully carved pews here. No patterned tiling floor. No ancient marble tombs. No stained-glass windows. Just bare earth, open walls, and a leaking roof to keep out the rain.

And the pulpit had no shiny brass eagle here. Sir Christopher Wren, it seemed, the great architect of St. Paul's, had never dropped in on Mayaland.

But like the Wednesday Communion service at St. Paul's, that afternoon was to become a very special time for me. We joined the people who had come to worship and to pray. So respectfully. So sincerely. Their village was under siege, their homes no longer their own. Too poor to build a structure of any substance, these men and women nevertheless found strength and solace in a simple place of worship. Where else could they go—but to the God they loved?

A small, rudely constructed wooden table formed the altar at the front of that little church. Draped over the table, in contrast to the brown of the dirt floor and the black of the timbers, was a spotlessly clean, white cloth. Roughly embroidered onto the cloth were words in the local language. I could not understand them but assumed they were a verse of Scripture. I wondered what it was. As I walked toward the front, I saw the small letters, "Hab. 2:20." And then I knew: "THE LORD IS IN HIS HOLY TEMPLE; LET ALL THE EARTH BE SILENT BEFORE HIM."

Anther time, another place. . . .

My wife says she is going to wear a leotard next time we visit. Worshiping there, she says, is a better workout than going to the gym. At the Verbo church in Quito, Ecuador, they are a lively crowd! In the extreme. There's a lot of action. And noise.

The psalmist tells us to make a joyful noise unto the Lord. Praise his name with dancing and make music to him with tambourine and harp. The people in many Latin American churches certainly do that! The Verbo people add a few extra guitars of all shapes and sizes, synthesizers, castanets, drums, and a whole host of other instruments. They sing enthusiastically. They clap. They "move." Young people run up and down the aisles waving banners. People hug. People laugh. People shout. People dance. There was an outward joy there that lightened our hearts and refreshed our spirits. It is so very . . . Latin. Nobody cared that the service went on for hours.

Standing in a worship service there one Sunday morning, I smiled as I recalled the church of my childhood in Sydney, Australia. Campsie Baptist certainly wasn't Latin! The men always wore dark suits; the women almost all wore hats. An old pump organ wheezed out the only accompaniment to stately old hymns from a denominational hymn-book. The service always started right at 11:00 A.M., and woe to the visiting preacher who went beyond 12:15 P.M.

As I thought about Campsie in the excitement of the Verbo church, I could affirm that both were very meaningful to me. But, oh, were they different.

How we enjoyed that Sunday in Quito! There was an undeniable sense of worship.

Another time, another place. . . .

I sat with profound respect in the balcony of the Moscow Baptist Church one Sunday morning in 1991. It was an old, rather tired-looking wooden building, quite small. I had not been able to find a seat among the crowd on the ground floor, but as I gazed down upon them from above, they looked so serious, even sad. A new Russia was beginning to emerge through cracks in the crust of oppressive communism that had prohibited worship among the population as a whole. But these people were of the old Russia. They were mainly women, the renowned babushkas of Moscow, simply dressed in their rather colorless Sunday best.

The music was harmonious and slow . . . and heavy.

As they had done over many years of oppression, they had gathered together to worship—in quiet defiance. These wonderful, heroic Christian women of Russia had a bond between them that the world outside could never understand.

Another time, another place. . . .

The lines of worshipers at a Muslim mosque deep in the heart of Islam move as one. From kneeling, they sway forward to place their foreheads on the carpet on the floor. Muslims at prayer. It happens like this all over the world. But today, in this place, some of those who bow pray in a very different way. They pray to God—through Jesus, in secret.

They have left their shoes at the door. They have come with their Muslim families and friends. They look no different to the thousands that have gathered to pray on bare carpeted floors under the gold minarets of the mosque. But they are different. They belong to Jesus.

Without denigrating the faith of their fathers, without separating themselves from family and community, they have come to see that the Jesus of the Quran is more than the Muslim holy book claims him to be. He is more than a prophet. He is God. He is that part of a divine trinity that came to earth to do more than "good." He came to be the Savior of the world. And they know him. Deeply. Personally.

But their very lives depend upon this remaining just what it is. A close, well-kept secret.

Christians in the West may not understand. They may not accept this ongoing connection with the mosque, that cultural centerpiece of the society in which they live. Even the very telling of their story will raise doubts about their salvation among some Western believers. Particularly those who know nothing of the stress under which these precious believers live.

But these Muslims do know Jesus. As one man described them to me—they are secret disciples.

There are secret disciples in the gospel narrative too.

Another time, another place. . . .

In 1961, I was an MAF pilot in Papua New Guinea. MAF's base and hangar were on one end of the Wirui airstrip at Wewak and the Divine Word Aviation Service, the flying arm of the Catholic Mission in the area, was on the other end. We helped each other out with spare parts when an airplane was unserviceable. We exchanged weather reports. We decided together who was more able to evacuate a patient when there was an emergency. But even there, they were Catholic and we were Protestant.

I was raised in an environment where the division between Protestants and Catholics created very real social barriers. I don't know, therefore, what my parents thought when I told them that one of my dearest friends in New Guinea was an American Catholic priest.

Father Ivo Reuter was the chief pilot for Divine Word. Ivo had arrived in New Guinea from Chicago in the early fifties as a newly ordained missionary priest, but his bishop sent him immediately to Australia to learn to fly so he could work in the aviation branch of the mission. "But I'm a missionary priest, my Lord," Ivo had said. Catholics are good at obedience, so Ivo learned to fly. When I last saw him, he was still a "flying priest" and had flown almost twenty thousand hours over the jungles and mountains of New Guinea.

I loved him as a dear friend, a brother in Christ.

We used to have wonderful, vigorous, yet friendly arguments about theology. Yes, we were different, in many ways. There were a number of very important things upon which we simply could not agree. We were poles apart in some aspects of theology and of practice. But those differences could never take away or dilute the wonder of the commonality Ivo and I shared. We affirmed to each other that our eternal salvation depended, totally, on our acceptance of Jesus and his death for us.

I saw Father Ivo in view of in his full clerical vestments only once. He looked fantastic!

I felt honored to be connected, in the Body, with Ivo Reuter.

Another time, another place....

We had enjoyed visiting this church. The building was pleasant, the lighting appropriate, the worship team polished and professional, the sermon—challenging but not pointing out our weaknesses too strongly. There was even coffee in the coffee shop by the foyer. There was a great feeling of fellowship and love in the place. People were friendly and made us feel most welcome.

This was North American evangelical Christianity!

"See you next week, folks," said the pastor as the service finished. He was casually dressed and smiling. "Can I ask you not to stay around too long? The folks coming for the next service are wanting in. They are certainly wanting your parking space! Thanks to all you guys who took part this morning, musicians, drama team, stewards, ushers. Don't forget the Wednesday night meeting in the chapel, the ladies' meeting Tuesday here in the sanctuary, the elders' meeting in my office Thursday. Saturday night, kids meet here at seven to go skating. And don't forget to come again next Sunday. Remember, I love you."

And so the service ended. The ushers had already counted the offering. Larger gifts were entered into the computer against member's names. After all, tax receipts are important. One of the men was matching the total offering figure against the budget, especially those gifts designated to the building fund.

People lined up in the foyer to buy a taped recording of the morning message. They each had someone in mind with whom they would like to share it. The bookshop was doing good business. People seemed as if they didn't want to leave. They stood around outside in the warm sunshine talking in groups.

Outside, helpers in orange vests guided traffic in and out of the huge parking lot. "God bless you, and have a nice day. Come back again," said one of them as we left. *We probably will*, I thought.

It had been a good morning. The machinery of the church was working well.

Another time, another place. . . .

"Good morning, precious saints of God," says the large African-American pastor. He rises to stand with open arms before the congregation to begin the Sunday morning service in suburban St. Louis in the United States. In typical African-American style they chorus back to him, "Good morning, precious saint of God."

What a great start to a service of worship and praise. The relationship is established. Horizontally between the many hundreds gathered in this almost all-black congregation. And vertically with the God they have come to worship. From all levels of society they have come. Young and old. Wealthy and poor. All beautifully dressed. Many of the ladies are wearing hats, a clear mark of respect for God.

They gather as equals. This is level ground. Joy fills the place.

And to me, their guest preacher, they reach out with great love and a smiling welcome. God is here with us! And the warmth of his love, shining through these marvelous people, penetrates to the depth of my soul.

The seventeen strangers in St. Paul's cathedral, the Guatemalan Indians in their primitive church, and joyful and enthusiastic Ecuadorians are all part of an invisible communion. Solemn, stoic Babushkas and silent, secretive Muslim Christians—they too are one, as part of this invisible communion. The Catholic priest in his white vestments, the parking attendant in his orange vest, and the African-American women with their wonderful Sunday hats—all of these and millions of others make up this glorious invisible communion. One body. One!

This communion is fraught with challenges, weakness, and the potential to fail. It is under threat, actively from those who would destroy it, passively from those who want its blessings without accepting its corresponding responsibilities. It so easily becomes insular and divided. It becomes noncaring and in great need of awakening and revival. Perhaps its greatest challenge is the propensity for its members to see themselves as stand-alone individual groups, with little desire to be united in spirit.

Jesus knew this. He loved its diversity right from its birth, but he knew the challenges that diversity brings. He prayed to the Father, with his "soul overwhelmed with sorrow to the point of death": "May they be brought to complete unity to let the world know that you sent me and have loved them even as you have loved me" (John 17:23).

God smiles upon this invisible communion, with its differences, with its superb diversity. ✶

Chapter Eighteen
···I Will Take Him from Here···

He tends his flock like a shepherd: He gathers the lambs in his arms and carries them close to his heart.

ISAIAH 40:11

* * *

Are not five sparrows sold for two pennies? Yet not one of them is forgotten by God. . . . Don't be afraid; you are worth more than many sparrows.

LUKE 12:6–7

The call on the airplane's radio caught my immediate attention:

"Bravo Victor Kilo, there is an urgent medical emergency at Nuku. Can you airlift a male patient to Wewak?"

Flying toward the coast on the return leg of a cargo flight to the highlands, I was within thirty or so miles of Nuku. Yes, I could make the diversion. From where I was I could see the hills to the south of Nuku.

Yes, I could do it . . . but . . .

This had been a busy day, and I was already running behind schedule. A medical emergency would really mess up the day. Flights would have to be cancelled or rescheduled to the already tight program of the following day.

As I turned away from my homeward track and reduced power for the descent ahead, frustration took priority over compassion. I wondered whether the patient really was ill enough to justify this disruption. Too often such flight requests had turned out not to be emergencies at all.

Descending overhead the small government outpost of Nuku in a tight turn, I could see a missionary friend standing at the top of the very steep hillside airstrip, a small human form lying on a stretcher beside him. No one else was there. As I landed and taxied the aircraft to where they were, I saw no movement from the still figure, even in response to the loud noise of the extra engine power needed to climb Nuku's steep airstrip and position the aircraft by the stretcher.

The small boy, perhaps ten or twelve years of age, was gravely ill.

He was also alone. No parent or guardian was there to travel with him.

Compassion took over from frustration, leaving me feeling guilty.

Barely conscious, the boy's startled eyes were filled with fear as I lifted him into the plane and laid him on the floor. There was no seat for him, and the crude stretcher upon which he had been carried to the airstrip could not fit into the aircraft. There was not even a mat to insulate his wasted and feverish body from the cold of the metal floor. The threadbare cloth wound around his thin body did little to help.

His brown face was almost white. Crusted mucus around his mouth and the salt of dried tears around his sunken eyes gave him a ghoulish appearance. But his eyes pierced my heart. They stared at me with a wordless appeal for help and mercy. His physical pain was compounded by fear, the total unknown of being placed in an airplane.

Terror and pain don't make a pretty face.

I couldn't tighten the cargo straps across his tiny chest. He was too small. As I bent over his little body to secure him as best I could, he made a moaning noise. His eyes closed. I was glad. He would be better off unconscious, I thought. The air was quite turbulent that day.

As I fastened my own seatbelt and readied the plane for takeoff, I knew that this was no false emergency. Gone were my concerns about passengers waiting for me on other airstrips. They would understand. This young New Guinean boy needed, and received, all my attention and concern.

Nuku airstrip at that time was no more than a very steep, grass-covered hill. I tried my best to avoid the bumps as the airplane accelerated down the slope, but the spring steel undercarriage of the Cessna made it very difficult.

I heard a quickly inhaled breath, and my young passenger winced as his little body was bounced about. I prayed, "Please help me find a smooth path for this kid." As soon as I was airborne, I climbed quickly to cruise at four thousand feet, above the level where the steamy, rising heat from the jungle below created turbulence.

To my departure call I added, "Request an ambulance on arrival. I have a seriously ill stretcher patient on board."

With the airplane trimmed for the forty-minute flight to the coast, I gave my full attention to my suffering passenger. I reached down and took his limp brown hand in mine. His face was still twisted with that same mixture of pain and fear, but responding to my touch, his eyes opened, slowly at first. He sighed deeply, and his lips moved to an ever so slight, tentative wisp of a smile.

We made a special connection in those moments, that boy and I.

We looked into each other's eyes. There was more than eye contact. Our hands were clasped together, but it was more than simply holding hands. Words weren't necessary, nor were they possible. Our communication was deeper, more profound. It was heart-to-heart, a blending of emotions. Pain was being covered with compassion, fear with love.

He didn't understand the words of my prayer as I prayed for him. But God did.

I knew that if any one of my five little boys at home were in such a precarious position, hundreds of people would pray for his healing. For this boy there was no one—but me. As I pleaded with God on his behalf, for life and for healing, the roaring of the engine may have overwhelmed the sound of my words, but it couldn't overwhelm my passion.

I felt his response. He seemed to marshal the minute amount of his remaining strength. He squeezed my hand. It wasn't strong. But I felt it. It seemed to say, "Thank you. Thank you for making me feel safe. Please don't let me go." He was not suffering alone.

We flew along in that bare little ambulance that day—holding hands!

I saw his brown eyes soften; I watched his fear begin to melt away. Replaced by calm. From the corners of his dry, cracked lips came a further, very slight movement. His weak smile, though still bearing the marks of pain, broadened. He returned my love. I know he did. His sunken eyes, ringed with that white salt of dried-up tears, were speaking to me, telling me he was glad that I was there.

God had heard and had answered my prayer. An immediate answer. Somehow, as through our hands we were physically connected, I knew that I was the connection, a true and certain connection, between heaven's love and this lonely, needy boy.

The air at that altitude was still, the weather good, requiring that I give only an occasional glance at the instruments and a quick scan of the sky outside. I kept eye contact with my little passenger. As the minutes went by, I spoke with him of God. Of healing. Of trust. As he squeezed my hand with the remnants of his almost depleted strength, I loved that kid as if he were my own.

The world would never know him, or notice—or even care. History would not record his life. He didn't stand tall even in his own village, nor in his nation. He didn't rate a guardian to accompany him to the hospital. Perhaps he was an orphan anyway.

He was just a sick little boy from the jungle. And he captured my heart.

But God also cared, and he had sent me along to be his agent of compassion to this frail, wasted child. This boy, made in the image of God, was of immense value. Many years before, Jesus had said, "Not even a sparrow shall fall to the ground without your father. You are of more value than many sparrows." This boy was not going to escape the Father's attention.

And so we flew on.

God answered my prayer for him that day, but not in the way I had so passionately requested. I had prayed that his life would be spared, that a period in the hospital under expert medical care would return him to full health.

A warm peace washed over his face, a face no longer ghoulish but somehow radiant.

I saw his eyes, which never left mine, slowly begin to glaze and lose their sight. They didn't close. His grip slowly lost its meager strength, and I watched the rhythm of his heaving chest slow down until there was no more movement. The little hand that had gripped mine became softly limp.

I watched that precious little kid die that day—with a smile on his face. And I cried.

I gently unclasped his lifeless hand and laid it on his now-still chest. I closed his eyes. They bore no more pain.

His body took on a particular dignity, lying there on the cold metal floor.

Something very special happened in that airplane as it flew on across the Sepik basin that day. Yes, there was a lifeless body there on the floor beside me. But there was another presence in that bare cabin. A holy presence. I felt it. I felt the presence of angels, almost the brush of their wings, as they came to collect a very precious life and gently carry it away.

My weeping was exchanged for a peculiar joy. I knew that the real life of that young Nuku boy, call it what you will, the soul, the spirit, had been taken through a glorious transition. He had gone through what the psalm describes as "the valley of the shadow of death." And I had the priceless honor of holding his hand as he walked through that valley. Another hand took him as he emerged on the other side, a new person with a glorious body.

I turned the airplane back toward Nuku. I just had to take him home. Trying not to let my emotion show I made a call, "I'm returning to Nuku, estimating there in twenty-five minutes. Please cancel request for an ambulance."

Thousands of years ago a prophet, calling the people to the challenge of declaring who God really is, said:

"Here is your God . . . He tends his flock like a shepherd. He gathers the lambs in his arms and carries them close to his heart."

The God of eternity, the creator of the universe—gathering lambs, giving them the highest priority? For some, that must be the greatest paradox. For others, for me and hopefully for you, it is the most wondrous thing.

God—a loving shepherd? Almost too much to believe!

I saw the Good Shepherd at work that day—in my airplane! He gathered that beautiful young boy into his arms and carried him close to his heart. Why? Because a young boy from Nuku is of great value to God, as great a value as any other boy that ever lived!

The blessing was for him, yes, but the blessing was for me as well.

Some may wonder and question, but I am convinced that I will meet my little friend in heaven one day. The experience of that day demands that I believe it. The answer to my prayer was far more than healing for him. It was wholeness. A heavenly, eternal transaction took place in that Cessna airplane at four thousand feet above the Sepik jungle. It was not a transaction of words. It was a transaction of Love.

God assigned to me the task of bringing him to the gates of heaven. He then said, "I will take him from here."

I will ask him his name when we meet. ✶

···A Note From the Author···

So, these are some of my stories. There are more that I may write at another time.

I write them for my own sake, to record for family and friends the profound privilege I have been afforded in life, for the privilege of making a difference in so many lives, in so many places. But I write them, above all, to share my absolute conviciton that indeed...

"There is no one like the God of Jeshurun, who rides on the heavens to help you and on the clouds in His majesty. The eternal God is your refuge, and underneath are the everlasting arms."

I learned that when I was very young and have never had cause to doubt it. I hope you have seen that wonderful truth . . . seen him, in these stories.

Mission Aviation Fellowship was formed soon after World War II to impact the world of mission, to bring development to the isolated and the poor, and to bring relief to the suffering through the use of aviation technology. MAF exists to "multiply the effectiveness of the church" as it reaches out with the Good News of the Gospel of Jesus Christ. In recent years, various aspects of Information Technology have been added to expand MAF's effectiveness even more.

Working in more than 35 countries around the world, MAF has utilized an aircraft fleet of more than 150 airplanes.

If you would like more information about MAF, contact:

MAF-USA:
P.O. Box 3202
Redlands, CA USA 92373-0998

MAF-Australia:
P.O. Box 211
Box Hill, Vic. 3128 Australia

MAF-Europe:
Focus House
Godington Road
Ashford, Kent. TN23 1HA
United Kingdom

MAF-Canada:
P.O. Box 368
Guelph, Ont. N1H 6K5
Canada

We want to hear from you. Please send your comments about this
book to us in care of the address below. Thank you.

ZondervanPublishingHouse
Grand Rapids, Michigan 49530
http://www.zondervan.com